LET'S EAT!

Let the world know that American cooking has come of age in these years of our Bicentennial and, with justified pride, let us read of, prepare, and enjoy the great and glorious recipes of our American heritage. *Come and get it! Join the crowd! Sit down to a meal!*

This is *our* food.

Dedicated to the Spirit of 1776—
Two Hundred Years Later.

BICENTENNIAL COOKBOOK

200 Years of Traditional American Recipes

Suzanne Topper

BELMONT TOWER BOOKS • NEW YORK CITY

A BELMONT TOWER BOOK

Published by

Tower Publications, Inc.
185 Madison Avenue
New York, N.Y. 10016

Printed in the United States of America.

THE BICENTENNIAL COOKBOOK

Table of Contents

Foreword

On May 10, 1776, Congress advised those colonies that had not already formed independent states, as Pennsylvania had already done, to set up such state governments. The thirteen colonies soon became thirteen United States of America to expand west, south, and north, until August 1959, when Hawaii followed Alaska's admission the previous January to swell our statehood to fifty.

In 1976, even those states that are noncontiguous with the forty-eight continental states share the history of the beginnings of this nation. As settlers of the original colony-states ventured westward, they brought with them grains and seeds as well as taste preferences for familiar foods. Settling anew in diverse, often inhospitable sections, carving civilization out of wilderness, they adapted to the local climate and vegetation. They farmed the land, bred livestock, and learned from Indian tribes methods of agriculture and animal husbandry, as well as new foods and ways of cooking. American cheeses, as great and sometimes greater than imported ones, evolved. Over the years, American ingenuity in the kitchen created delicacies from Coney Island red hots to Western enchiladas. Today Thanksgiving turkey is a traditional national favorite, far removed in both years and territory from the first Thanksgiving. The wild turkey, once plentiful in North America, exists only in limited ranges, and our domestic turkey is a bird of a different feather.

Just as the accents of speech underwent changes according to locale, so did our tastes in food. Inevitably, regionally favored recipes came into being. The purpose of this book is to present a representative sampling of the wide variety of American recipes as an enduring tribute to our hardiness as a nation over two hundred years.

This, then, is a tribute to our country's founding fathers and to their vision of its endurability and its strength. Fortified by the foods they enjoy, Americans must currently renew their faith in that wonderfully unique experiment of 1776—the United States of America, which has endured and shall continue to do so.

Americans have too often deprecated their native recipes. Both those who have traveled abroad and those who have remained at home frequently believe that the choicest cuisine is foreign. Read, prepare, and enjoy the wonderful native recipes of our country and you will find that American cooking is no lesser art. While it is, of course, true that what we recognize as American recipes have often had foreign beginnings, in usage these recipes have undergone adaptations and have emerged as solely American dishes.

Let us take pride in our nation and in our foods.

Colonial Food

By 1776, some foods in America had already become traditional. These were not purely Indian concoctions, but bona fide colonial recipes. Game was plentiful in the forests. Fish abounded in rivers, brooks, and ponds, some species joyfully leaping high out of the water as if teasing the fishermen to catch them. In the ocean waters, more than two hundred varieties of fish awaited nets and a baited hook. Even so, out of ignorance of the methods of survival in the wilderness and lack of the hunting-for-sport experience of the cupper classes, the Pilgrims would all have died of starvation during their first winter on these shores had not friendly Indians supported them with their maize. It is curious that although the forests of Northeastern America were home to wild turkeys, the first Thanksgiving feast probably did not include this bird on the bill on fare.

Later settlers, more knowledgeable than the

Pilgrims had been, soon hunted the succulent birds until they now exist only in heavily wooded areas.

Our shopping centers have modern supermarkets which stock all variety of prepared convenience foods, as well as a spectacular selection of foods grown and bred over the wide reaches of this nation, and beyond. Our modern kitchens couldn't have been imagined by our forebears as they labored in their kitchens with wide stone fireplaces for cooking while the inefficient chimneys allowed smoke to seep into the rooms, redden their eyes, and cling to their hair and clothes.

At that time, skillets, fashioned with long legs to stand on hot coals, served as griddles and fry pans. Supplanting less efficient metal pots, heavy-weight cast iron pots were utilized in preparation of meals. Often these hung on chains from wooden lug poles. Yankee ingenuity devised a crane from which to hang the pots. Many meals, such as stews, or meat boiled with pudding, were cooked in a single pot. Porridge was also cooked in these pots. This method of cooking (multiple foods in one pot) grew in popularity because the food, once in the pot, needed little tending and provided a slight respite for the goodwife as she provided her family with hearty, nourishing meals.

A Dutch oven such as we use today is not the same as the lidded, wide, long-legged kettle that rested on the coals or on the stone hearth when not in use. To its insides were consigned potatoes or other vegetables for cooking, or dough for bread. It was called an oven because it stood on the coals but also had hot coals piled high around it and heaped across the cover.

The earliest settlers used wooden trenchers for plates. These were long, carved of wood, and double-purposed. By turning the underside up once the main course was consumed, a clean surface was presented for dessert. This might be pudding, pie, or cake. Usually, adults sat on stools to eat and children ate standing. Engaged couples enjoyed their meals from the same trencher.

Pewter was used as a table metal for cups, but there were no niceties of table service in the American wilderness in the 1600s. There was no silverware, china, or glass. Indeed, no forks were generally used—fingers sufficed. There was also the ingenious use of a clam shell for scooping food into the mouth. Knives and napkins completed the table setting.

Seasonings were introduced and became important in recipes. Kitchen gardens, consisting of herbal plants, became popular and were carefully tended. In this primitive society, there was a uniformly high standard of politeness. This chiefly involved the use of napkins. An early etiquette book advised that the napkin should not be "foul all over, but at one corner."

The rustic general store was a place for barter as well as original purchase. It was also the closest imitation of a club then existent in rural areas. Here, gossip was related, tall tales told, and politics discussed. Here, too, was the hub of patriotism—that infectious fever that bound colonists, farmers, and frontiermen into one force until, through travail, war, and blind abiding faith, all eventually became charter citizens of one of the thirteen colonies, that became the United States of America.

It wasn't until the 1700s that regional cooking evidenced itself in America. Southern cookery developed in diverse ways. There were both Creole cooking, a blend of Spanish, English, some French, and West African cuisines, and the French culinary school that imparted sophistication to Virginia cooking. Wines were much favored at meals, and rich combinations of foods became a habit on tables set with linen clothes, polished silver, and gleaming crystal in wealthy homes, as well as on less wealthy tables to the best of the owner's ability.

By the early 1800s, American food and tastes were under much scrutiny and criticism. The delicate cooking of early Virginia had deteriorated with spoiling foods, much of it ill-prepared. By contrast, the Pennsylvania Dutch people ate more wholesomely and enjoyed their deliciously prepared recipes.

Similarly, the Shakers were adept at devising recipes and preparing choice food. Shaker sects pioneered new settlements from the East into the Midwest.

In the breadbasket of Kansas, the land supported wheat, and in Iowa the soil's fertility nourished the roots of food crops. The plains states of Nebraska, the Dakotas, Kansas, Oklahoma, Minnesota, and the eastern portions of Wyoming and Washington fed their inhabitants with an endless bounty of wheat and became the range for livestock.

As the railroad pushed westward and transported foods beyond their native locales, Chicago became the hub of business transactions, and the city's slaughtering and packing plants made it the ultimate destination of herds of livestock.

In the Southwest, Mexican and Indian influences gave fiery taste to the native foodstuffs. In other areas, ethnic flavors imparted interesting flavor touches to locally consumed foods, as in German recipes enjoyed in Milwaukee, St. Louis, Cincinnati, and some neighborhoods of Chicago. The treatment of ethnic cooking would require more space than this volume can give it.

Southeastern cooking doubtless owes much to the skills of black slaves, and it isn't at all coincidental that a startling similarity exists between Creole and West African recipes.

In the Northeast, each wave of immigrants brought with them the knowledge of unfamiliar foods, and this ultimately widened the choice on our national menu. New York was called the melting pot. More than deserving of this definition on the basis of humanity settling in the city, quite literally the pots of its inhabitants wafted aromas of unusual, soon to be generally accepted, foods that widened the culinary horizons of all Americans.

In the far West, San Francisco, then the most cosmopolitan of cities, whose sole flaw was the fault she wore under her petticoats in the bowels of the earth, Chinese immigrants settled in their own district of the city. They brought with them their own gastronomy, using sharks' fins and birds' nests. This geological fault underlying San Francisco runs inland parallel to the Pacific coast and churns up minerally rich soil that harbors vineyards and orchards of lush fruits. California is the salad state, where the salad is given such importance as to be eaten in a separate course before the main dish is brought to table.

California has drawn people from all of the other 49 states, although some have fled the state in fear of earthquake rumblings and predictions. In its foods, California is nothing if not cosmopolitan, and has contributed Chinese, Armenian, and Mexican recipes of renown, just as Italian-Americans have contributed pasta, and Jewish cooks their gefilte fish. However, as stated earlier, this book does not offer recipes that are distinctively foreign. Surely, people who have immigrated to the United States feel at home with their own cookery—the purpose of the *Bicentennial Cookbook* is to present as wholly American recipes as is possible and, while this cannot always be entirely guaranteed, it nevertheless seems best to omit such recipes as veal parmesan and Indian curries.

Let the world know that American cooking has come of age in these years of our Bicentennial and, with justified pride, let us read of, prepare, and enjoy the great and glorious recipes of our American heritage. *Come and get it! Join the crowd! Sit down to a meal!*

THIS IS *OUR* FOOD.

Original Colonial Menus

Although the early colonists in the Jamestown settlement were surrounded by the bounty of their new land, they suffered starvation because they weren't able to harvest the crops they had farmed and did not know how to hunt or fish. It was only after many of their company had starved, that they learned techniques that would assure them a full supply of food. They learned how to smoke some of their meats to preserve them, how to bake under primitive conditions at the open kitchen hearth, and how to cook fine foods in their iron kettles. Their meals were simply prepared, but hearty and delicious.

At that time, recipes began at the very beginning—and the first instruction was how to obtain the food. The pot always contained enough for seconds or for an unexpected wayfarer, who was glad to put aside his sustaining johnnycake, sit at the side of his host, and partake of the meal at a wooden trough or plain board table.

Consider these instructions:

Catch a young turkey, kill it by strangulation, pluck and cleanse it. Take one large kettle and fill with clear water from a running stream. Remove apples, onions, and carrots from cellar, wash, then cut up. Put all into pot with bird. Place pot close over hot coals, maintaining steady heat. Cook several hours, and let hang over hearth until dinner.

As the Colonies prospered, sophistication of taste and recipes developed. From original exchange of recipes among goodwives, the concept of recipe collections or cookbooks emerged—and these were not always authored by women.

For breakfast, there would be cereal, ladled in lavish servings; four or more eggs, usually poached; home-baked breads; and tea or beer (yes, beer at breakfast!). It should be noted that beer was regularly consumed by children, as milk was a danger until pasteurization came into use. In fact, many years after the Revolutionary period, Abraham Lincoln's mother succumbed to "the milk sickness."

The midday meal, the largest of the day, was likely to offer a steaming soup, rich and flavorful with meat and vegetables. In addition, there might be another meat, game fowl, or fish from close-by streams; vegetables from the garden or the cellar; certainly a relish, if not two; and a hearty dessert pudding. Perhaps several glasses of treasured European wine were quaffed, or one made at home was served. And, then, there was always the beer.

Supper was sometimes some of the dishes leftover from the large midday meal, with another fresh batch of bread. Bedtime came early for adult as well as child, and often the following day's breakfast came before the rooster's first crowing.

Our Fifty States

ALABAMA

Statehood: December 14, 1819.
Motto: We dare defend our rights.
Nicknames: Cotton State, Heart of Dixie.
Food production: Hogs, peanuts, soybeans, cattle, corn.

ALASKA

Statehood: January 3, 1959.
Motto: North to the future.
Nicknames: The Last Frontier, Land of the Midnight Sun, Great Land.
Food production: Fish, dairy, cattle, vegetables.

ARIZONA

Statehood: February 14, 1912.
Motto: God enriches.
Nicknames: Apache State, Grand Canyon State.
Food production: Cattle, dairy, lettuce.

ARKANSAS

Statehood: June 15, 1836.
Motto: Let the people rule.
Nickname: Land of Opportunity.
Food production: Poultry, cattle, soybeans, rice.

CALIFORNIA

Statehood: September 9, 1850.
Motto: Eureka, I have found it.
Nickname: Golden State.
Food production: Vegetables, fruits, wine, rice, seafood.

COLORADO

Statehood: August 1, 1876.
Motto: Nothing without providence.
Nickname: Centennial State.
Food production: Cattle, sheep, dairy, sugar beets.

CONNECTICUT

(One of the original thirteen colonies.)

Statehood: January 9, 1788.
Motto: He who transplanted, sustains.
Nicknames: Constitution State, Nutmeg State.
Food production: Dairy.

DELAWARE

(One of the original thirteen colonies.)

Statehood: December 7, 1787.
Motto: Liberty and independence.
Nicknames: Diamond State, First State.
Food production: Shellfish, apples, peaches, corn, soybeans, potatoes.

FLORIDA

Statehood: March 3, 1845.
Motto: In God we trust.
Nicknames: Peninsula State, Sunshine State.
Food production: Citrus fruits, nuts, cattle, dairy, shellfish.

GEORGIA

(One of the original thirteen colonies.)

Statehood: January 2, 1788.
Motto: Wisdom, justice, moderation.
Nicknames: Empire State of the South, Peach State.
Food production: Peaches, peanuts, cattle, eggs, corn.

HAWAII

Statehood: August 21, 1959.
Motto: The life of the land is perpetuated in righteousness.
Nicknames: Aloha State, Paradise of the Pacific.
Food production: Pineapples, deepwater fish, livestock, sugar.

IDAHO

Statehood: July 3, 1890.
Motto: It is forever.
Nicknames: Gem State, Potato State.
Food production: Potatoes, sheep, dairy, sugar beets, cattle, wheat.

ILLINOIS

Statehood: December 3, 1818.
Motto: State sovereignty, national union.

Nickname: Prairie State.
Food production: Hogs, cattle, dairy, corn, soybeans, wheat.

INDIANA

Statehood: December 11, 1816.
Motto: The crossroads of America.
Nickname: Hoosier State.
Food production: Corn, grain, tomatoes, soybeans, hogs, cattle, dairy.

IOWA

Statehood: December 28, 1846.
Motto: Our liberties we prize, our rights we will maintain.
Nickname: Hawkeye State.
Food production: Corn, hogs, cattle, dairy, soybeans.

KANSAS

Statehood: January 29, 1861.
Motto: To the stars through difficulties.
Nicknames: Sunflower State, Jayhawk State.
Food production: Grains, eggs, cattle, hogs, sorghum.

KENTUCKY

Statehood: June 1, 1792.
Motto: United we stand, divided we fall.
Nickname: Blue Grass State.
Food production: Corn, cattle, hogs, dairy.

LOUISIANA

Statehood: April 30, 1812.

Motto: Union, justice, confidence.
Nicknames: Pelican State, Creole State, Sugar State.
Food production: Sweet potatoes, sugar cane, rice, shrimp, oysters.

MAINE

Statehood: March 15, 1820.
Motto: I direct.
Nickname: Pine Tree State.
Food production: Potatoes, lobster, clams, dairy, apples.

MARYLAND

(One of the original thirteen colonies.)

Statehood: April 28, 1788.
Motto: Manly deeds, womanly words.
Nicknames: Free State, Old Line State.
Food production: Fish, oysters, corn, wheat, dairy, crabs, clams, cattle.

MASSACHUSETTS

(One of the original thirteen colonies.)

Statehood: February 6, 1788.
Motto: By the sword we seek peace, but peace only under liberty.
Food production: Fish, dairy, poultry, vegetables.

MICHIGAN

Statehood: January 26, 1837.
Motto: If you seek a pleasant peninsula, look around you.
Nickname: Wolverine State.
Food production: Dairy, table grapes, cherries, sugar beets, cattle, poultry, corn, wheat.

MINNESOTA

Statehood: May 11, 1858.
Motto: The star of the north.
Nicknames: Gopher State, Land of 10,000 Lakes, North Star State.
Food production: Wheat, barley, rye, cattle, hogs, dairy items, corn, soybeans.

MISSISSIPPI

Statehood: December 10, 1817.
Motto: By virtue and arms.
Nickname: Magnolia State.
Food production: Pecans, soybeans, cattle, shrimp, oysters.

MISSOURI

Statehood: August 10, 1821.
Motto: The welfare of the people shall be the supreme law.
Nickname: Show Me State.
Food production: Cattle, hogs, soybeans.

MONTANA

Statehood: November 8, 1889.
Motto: Gold and silver.
Nickname: Treasure State.
Food production: Sheep, wheat, barley, cattle, dairy.

NEBRASKA

Statehood: March 1, 1867.
Motto: Equality before the law.
Nicknames: Cornhusker State, Beef State.
Food production: Cattle, hogs, corn, grains, sugar beets.

NEVADA

Statehood: October 31, 1864.
Motto: All for our country.
Nicknames: Sagebrush State, Silver State.
Food production: Sheep, cattle, wheat.

NEW HAMPSHIRE

(One of the original thirteen colonies.)

Statehood: June 21, 1788.
Motto: Live free or die.
Nickname: Granite State.
Food production: Dairy, apples, potatoes.

NEW JERSEY

(One of the original thirteen colonies.)

Statehood: December 18, 1787.
Motto: Liberty and prosperity.
Nickname: Garden State.
Food production: Eggs, vegetables.

NEW MEXICO

Statehood: January 6, 1912.
Motto: It grows as it goes.
Nicknames: Land of Enchantment, Sunshine State.
Food production: pecans, peanuts, lettuce, apples.

NEW YORK

(One of the original thirteen colonies.)

Statehood: July 26, 1788.
Motto: Ever upward.
Nickname: Empire State.
Food production: Livestock, wine, apples, vegetables, dairy.

NORTH CAROLINA

(One of the original thirteen colonies.)

Statehood: November 21, 1789.
Motto: To be, rather than to seem.
Nickname: Tar Heel State.
Food production: Corn, peanuts, shrimp, crabs.

NORTH DAKOTA

Statehood: November 2, 1889.
Motto: Liberty and union, now and forever, one and inseparable.
Nicknames: Sioux State, Flickertail State.
Food production: Wheat, rye, livestock, potatoes, dairy.

OHIO

Statehood: March 1, 1803.
Motto: With God, all things are possible.
Nickname: Buckeye State.
Food production: Wheat, corn, livestock.

OKLAHOMA

Statehood: November 16, 1907.
Motto: Labor conquers all.
Nickname: Sooner State.
Food production: Corn, cattle, grains.

OREGON

Statehood: February 14, 1859.
Motto: The Union.
Nickname: Beaver State.
Food production: Sheep, fruits, nuts, salmon, tuna, crabs.

PENNSYLVANIA

(One of the original thirteen colonies.)

Statehood: December 12, 1787.
Motto: Virtue, liberty, and independence.
Nickname: Keystone State.
Food production: Corn, oats, wheat, dairy.

RHODE ISLAND

(One of the original thirteen colonies.)

Statehood: May 29, 1790.
Motto: Hope.
Nicknames: Gunflint State, Little Rhody.
Food production: Dairy, poultry.

SOUTH CAROLINA

(One of the original thirteen colonies.)

Statehood: May 23, 1788.
Mottoes: Prepared in mind and resources. While I breathe, I hope.
Nickname: Palmetto State.
Food production: Shellfish.

SOUTH DAKOTA

Statehood: November 2, 1889.
Motto: Under God the people rule.
Nicknames: Coyote State, Sunshine State.
Food production: Cattle, grains, hogs, corn.

TENNESSEE

Statehood: June 1, 1796.
Motto: America at its best.
Nickname: Volunteer State.
Food production: Corn, cattle, hogs, dairy.

TEXAS

Statehood: December 29, 1845.
Motto: Friendship.
Nickname: Lone Star State.
Food production: Wheat, corn, cattle, pecans, sheep, swine.

UTAH

Statehood: January 4, 1896.
Motto: Industry.
Nickname: Beehive State.
Food production: Vegetables, fruits, turkeys, cattle, wheat.

VERMONT

Statehood: March 4, 1791.
Motto: Freedom and unity.
Nickname: Green Mountain State.
Food production: Maple syrup, dairy, apples.

VIRGINIA

(One of the original thirteen colonies.)
Statehood: June 25, 1788.
Motto: Thus always to tyrants.
Nicknames: The Old Dominion, Mother of Presidents.
Food production: Fruits, corn, livestock, dairy.

WASHINGTON

Statehood: November 11, 1889.
Motto: By and by.
Nicknames: Evergreen State, Chinook State.
Food production: Apples, fish, wheat, cattle, poultry.

WEST VIRGINIA

Statehood: June 20, 1863.
Motto: Mountaineers are always free.
Nickname: Mountain State.
Food production: Cattle, dairy, apples, corn.

WISCONSIN

Statehood: May 29, 1848.
Motto: Forward.
Nicknames: Badger State, Cheese State.
Food production: Cheese, dairy, vegetables, beer.

WYOMING

Statehood: July 10, 1890.
Motto: Equal rights.
Nickname: Equality State.
Food production: Sheep, sugar beets, cattle, grains.

Official Bicentennial Sites

Although this is a cookbook, it does celebrate the American Bicentennial and, as such, it is appropriate to make mention of those sites designated by the United States government as Official Bicentennial Sites. These are not to be confused with America's historic landmarks, which dot the entire nation:

Mount Rushmore National Memorial, South Dakota

Located in the Black Hills, in the Southwest portion of the state, twenty-five miles from Rapid City, is the world-famed mountain carving of the busts of George Washington, Thomas Jefferson, Abraham Lincoln, and Theodore Roosevelt. Authorized in 1925 by an act of Congress, it wasn't completed until the mid-1940s. The sculptor was Gutzon Borglum; upon his death, his son Lincoln completed the massive and enduring work.

George Rogers Clark National Historical Park, Indiana

This park commemorates the winning of the Northwest Territory and perpetuates the name of Clark in this recreation area along the banks of the Wabash River, near Vincennes.

Fort McHenry National Monument and Historic Shrine, Maryland

Located in Baltimore, this was constructed between the years 1798 and 1803. It was during the War of 1812 that the defense of Fort McHenry inspired Francis Scott Key to write The Star Spangled Banner. *Key witnessed the bombardment of the fort by the British fleet. Toward dawn, when the guns ceased firing, the fort was intact and the Stars and Stripes still flew.*

Cowpens National Battlefield, South Carolina

On this ground, 18 miles northeast of Spartanburg, the American forces achieved a significant victory over the British in the Carolina Campaign of 1781.

Fort Moultrie (Fort Sumter National Monument), South Carolina

On June 28, 1776, 400 patriots defeated a British squadron of nine ships. This victory delayed British operations in the South. The fort is located near Fort Sumter, on Sullivan's Island in Charleston harbor.

Kings Mountain National Military Park, South Carolina

In the mountain countryside south of Kings Mountain, the frontiermen struck a blow for freedom on October 7, 1780. The mountain men knew how to operate in the rugged terrain and, against repeated bayonet charges, they closed in on the Loyalist forces to take the ridge and hold the mountain summit.

Federal Hall National Memorial, New York

Located on Wall and Nassau Streets in New York City, this was the site of the Stamp Act Congress of 1765. Here also was housed the Federal government, and George Washington was inaugurated on this location in Federal Hall as the first President of the United States. In 1789, the Bill of Rights was voted on in Federal Hall.

Fort Stanwix National Monument, New York

In 1777, Patriot forces vanquished a British invasion from Canada. This defeat for the British contributed to the American victory at Saratoga. The Monument is in Rome, New York.

Hamilton Grange National Memorial, New York

This home, once the residence of Alexander Hamilton, is located on Convent Avenue in upper Manhattan.

Saratoga National Historic Park, New York

This is the site of an American victory over the British in 1777. The battle was a significant turning point in the Revolutionary War, since it led to recognition and assistance from France. The scene of past battle is several miles south of Schuyler.

Statue of Liberty National Monument, New York

Erected on Liberty Island in New York Harbor, the statue was a gift from France for the American Centennial in 1876. Housed in the base of the statue is the American Museum of Immigration.

Adams National Historic Site, Massachusetts

The Adams mansion, homestead of the Adams family, is located in Quincy. John Adams purchased the home in 1787 and lived out his life here.

Minute Man National Historic Park, Massachusetts

This is the site of the initial resistance of Colonials against British regulars on April 19, 1775. Included in the park are famed North Bridge, the Minute Man Statue, and four miles of Battle Road between Lexington and Concord.

Salem Maritime National Historic Site, Massachusetts

This site commemorates the maritime history of the United States from the 17th through the 19th centu-

ry. Salem was the port for blockade-running vessels during the Revolution and was also a site for shipbuilding. To see are the Custom House, circa 1819; the Derby House, built in 1762, a merchants home; and Derby Wharf, where captured goods were privateered from British ships during the Revolution and supplies provided for the Continental Army. During the War of 1812, the wharf was again active as a center of shipping.

Fort Necessity National Battlefield, Pennsylvania

Here, in 1754, Lt. Col. George Washington surrendered his company to French troops and Indians in the opening battle of the French and Indian War. Although the French subsequently burned the Colonial fort, old documents and archaeological diggings have enabled an exact replica to be built of the fort, its entrenchments, and earthworks. It is located eleven miles east of Uniontown.

Hopewell Village National Historic Site, Pennsylvania

Here, a few miles south of Birdsbors, stands an ironworks in operation during the Revolution. From here, also, desperately needed flour was shipped to Washington and his troops at Valley Forge in 1778.

Independence National Historic Park, Pennsylvania

In the heart of downtown Philadelphia, on Walnut Street, this was the scene of much of America's early history. Independence Hall and the Liberty Bell are situated here, and the First and Second Continental

Congresses met here in 1774 and 1775. Here, too, the Declaration of Independence was drafted and approved in 1776 and the Constitution of the United States drawn up in 1787. Our Federal Government was located here for ten years.

Guilford Courthouse National Military Park, North Carolina

Here Cornwallis exacted a devastating victory over American forces in 1781. The battle was furiously fought and, although the British were victors, more than one-fourth of their forces were killed. Subsequently, in 1781, Cornwallis surrendered in Yorktown. The park is on the outskirts of Greensboro.

Moores Creek National Military Park, North Carolina

In 1776, on this site, northwest of Wilmington, Delaware, the Patriots achieved a significant victory over a larger Loyalist force, thereby blocking a British thrust toward the southern colonies.

Nelson House (Colonial National Historic Park), Virginia

Located in Yorktown, this was the home of Thomas Nelson, Jr., a signer of the Declaration of Independence. The grounds encompass most of Jamestown, site of the first permanent English settlement in the New World. Here, on October 19, 1781, the British formally surrendered, ending the Revolutionary War.

George Washington Birthplace National Monument, Virginia

George Washington was born on this plantation, on the shores of the Potomac River, on February 22, 1732. This small house is not to be confused with Mount Vernon, which is also located along the Potomac.

Morristown National Historic Park, New Jersey

This was the site of the main encampment of the Continental Army in the winters of 1777-1778 and 1779-1780. During this time of cold and insufficient food, George Washington worked to reorganize his tattered, frostbitten, weary, and depleted troups.

National Capital Area, District of Columbia

The following locations in Washington are designated Bicentennial sites: the Mall, extending from the Capitol grounds to the Lincoln Memorial; Washington Monument, the 555-feet high obelisk; Potomac Park, famed for spring-blooming cherry trees; the Chesapeake and Ohio Canal, a former important waterway, planned by George Washington, but not begun until 1828 (in 1924 the canal was severely damaged by floods and today is no more than a historic curiosity); Anacostia Park, on the Anacostia River where, in 1608, Captain John Smith founded the Indian Village of Nacotchtank; the Thomas Jefferson Memorial, a circular domed building on the east side of the Potomac River, across from Washington, D.C.; and finally, the inspiring Lincoln Memorial, which was dedicated in 1922.

During this Bicentennial period and beyond, the food on our tables can be every bit as traditional as these places in our nation's history. Knowing and enjoying our forefathers' recipes is not only a tribute to their valor, but also an opportunity to partake of history.

Soup and Chowders

KALE SOUP

(Martha's Vineyard)

This recipe is Portugese in heritage.

cracked marrow bone
1/2 pound beef chuck (remove fat)
1 bay leaf
1-1/2 teaspoons salt
freshly ground pepper
1/3 teaspoon garlic powder
2 medium onions, chopped coarsely
1 bunch fresh kale
3 large potatoes, pared and diced
1/2 pound spiced sausage (if you can't obtain authentic Portugese sausage, any kind will do)

In a deep saucepan over low heat, simmer marrow bone, beef, bay leaf, salt, pepper, garlic powder, onions, kale, and potatoes in water to cover. Allow to simmer 1-1/2 hours. Dice the sausage into very small pieces and add it to the saucepan. Remove marrow bone and simmer 30 minutes more.

This is a nourishing, interesting soup, hearty enough to serve with just a crusty bread and a salad, although traditionally it would be followed by a fish or seafood dish.

Serves 4 to 6

TOMATO-CORN CHOWDER

(Southwest)

2 slices bacon, fried and crumbled
4 potatoes, pared and cubed
1 tablespoon onion powder
1 cup canned tomatoes, with liquid
1-1/2 cups water
2 cups milk
2 cups corn kernels
1 teaspoon salt
freshly ground pepper
dash of hot pepper sauce
paprika

Place bacon, potatoes, onion powder, tomatoes and liquid in water in large saucepan over moderate heat. Bring to a boil, then reduce heat to simmer. While stirring well, add milk, then corn kernels, and season with salt, pepper, and hot pepper sauce. Continue to simmer 40 minutes, or until potatoes are very soft. Mash potatoes in pot with a spoon. If liquid has reduced appreciably, add a bit more milk. Dust each serving with paprika for color and flavor.

Serves 4

PRETZEL SOUP

(Pennsylvania Dutch)

Some people eat pretzels heavily in hot weather for the salt. Others enjoy pretzels anytime and, as with munching peanuts, can't stop eating them. There are some who enjoy pretzels with beer, but for those who've imbibed too much beer or another potent beverage, such people say this soup helps.

2 tablespoons flour
2 tablespoons butter or margarine
4 cups milk
freshly ground pepper
1 tablespoon chopped parsley
12 large pretzels, broken up

In a deep saucepan over low flame, brown the flour in butter or margarine. Gradually add milk, then add pepper. Stir constantly. Heat to just below boiling point. Lower heat and add parsley. Place broken pretzels in soup bowls. Ladle soup over pretzels. Serve hot.

Serves 4

PHILADELPHIA PEPPER POT SOUP

(Pennsylvania)

The American appetite has rarely invented new dishes that don't reflect ethnic beginnings, whether foreign or Indian. Usually purely American recipes were formulated with ingenuity to meet an emergency, as in Valley Forge when, in the dreadful winter of 1777 to 1778, a cook under orders from General Washington devised a tempting dish out of little. Proud of his creation, he named it for his native Philadelphia.

1 pound honeycomb tripe, washed under running water
2 beef bouillon cubes
small quantity of any cooked leftover meat
1 marrowbone, cracked
1 teaspoon salt
1 large onion, minced
1/2 cup celery, chopped
1 bay leaf
1/2 teaspoon thyme
2 medium carrots, scraped and sliced in 1/2-inch lengths
2 medium potatoes, pared and diced
10 peppercorns
3 whole cloves
1/2 cup light cream

Place tripe and at least 3 quarts of water in a deep saucepan. Cook over moderate heat until boiling point is reached. Reduce heat and allow tripe to simmer about 7 hours over low heat. When the tripe is tender, remove to a cutting board and mince it. Retain water remaining in saucepan and add beef bouillon cubes. Return tripe to saucepan with leftover cooked meat, cut in small pieces. Add marrowbone, salt, onion, celery, bay leaf, thyme, carrots, potatoes, peppercorns, and cloves. If remaining water is less than 6 cups, add water to compensate. Simmer over low heat for 40 minutes, or until vegetables are fully tender. In a small saucepan, heat cream over low heat, then gradually stir into the soup. Remove bay leaf, peppercorns, and cloves before serving.

Serves 6

PEANUT SOUP

(Virginia)

1/2 cup roasted peanuts (unsalted)
3 cups beef bouillon
1 cup light cream
1 teaspoon salt
1 tablespoon brown sugar
1/4 teaspoon ginger
1/2 teaspoon nutmeg (ground)

Cook peanuts in bouillon in a saucepan over moderate heat for 25 minutes, or until nuts are tender. Stir in cream and flavor with salt, brown sugar, and ginger. Reduce heat and simmer for 20 minutes. Top each serving with a dusting of nutmeg.

Serves 4

TERRAPIN SOUP

(Delaware, Algonquin Indians)

Terrapin is the name given the American turtle, which the Indians enjoyed before it became more generally recognized as a delicacy.

1 pound canned or frozen terrapin meat
3 leeks with tops, chopped
3 cups beef bouillon
2-1/2 cups water
1/2 teaspoon onion powder
1/2 teaspoon salt
freshly ground pepper
juice of 1/2 lemon

Place the terrapin in a deep saucepan with all other ingredients, and simmer, covered, for approximately 4 hours. At that time, remove meat, cut into small pieces, and return to soup pot. If liquid is drastically reduced in quantity, add more beef bouillon or water. Allow to simmer once again, covered, 1/2 to 3/4 hour longer, depending on the tenderness of the terrapin.

Serves 4

TURTLE SOUP

(Kentucky)

3 tablespoons butter or margarine
2 medium onions, chopped
2-1/2 tablespoons flour
1-1/2 quarts water
3 beef bouillon cubes, or 3 packages beef concentrate
2 medium carrots, scraped and sliced
2 medium potatoes, pared and cut in pieces
1 teaspoon salt
freshly ground pepper
1 10-ounce can turtle meat, diced
1 tablespoon lemon juice
1 tablespoon Worcestershire sauce
1 cup sherry
2 hard-boiled eggs, sliced

Using a large, deep saucepan, melt butter over low heat. Add onions, then flour, while stirring constantly. Pour in water and add beef bouillon cubes, while continuing to stir. Add carrots and potatoes. Season with salt and pepper. After simmering 1-1/2 hours, add turtle meat, lemon juice, and Worcestershire sauce. Continue simmering 10 minutes. Then stir in sherry and, after 5 more minutes, remove from heat. Garnish each serving with slices of egg, floated on the surface.

Serves 6

CORN CHOWDER

(Iowa)

This recipe is from the heart of the Corn-belt.

2 cups corn kernels, fresh or canned
2 slices bacon, fried and crumbled
1 medium onion, finely chopped
2 medium potatoes, diced
2 cups water
freshly ground pepper
1-1/2 cups milk, scalded
1-1/2 tablespoons flour
1 tablespoon butter or margarine
paprika

Place corn, bacon, onion, and potatoes in water and cook over low heat, simmering 15 minutes, or until potatoes are tender. Season with salt and pepper, and gradually stir in scalded milk, then the flour, a little at a time so that it will not be lumpy. Continue stirring for about 4 or 5 minutes more. Add butter and mix thoroughly. By this time, the chowder will be thickening as it begins to boil. Serve hot in old-fashioned soup bowls (from a tureen at the table, if possible) and dust each serving with paprika. A crusty bread goes well with this hearty soup.

Serves 6

KING CRAB SOUP

(Alaska)

Whether or not you can obtain the authentic Alaskan king crab, this recipe is royalty among soups.

2 cups chicken broth
2 cups cooked crab meat, flaked
3 egg yolks, lightly beaten
2 cups milk
1 teaspoon salt
generous amount freshly ground pepper
1 tablespoon Worcestershire sauce
1/2 cup fresh mushrooms, sliced
1 cup heavy cream
2 teaspoons parsley flakes

Simmer chicken broth in a deep saucepan and add crab meat. Slowly stir in egg yolks. Continue constant stirring as you add milk and season with salt, pepper, and Worcestershire sauce. Be careful to maintain the lowest heat. Stir in mushrooms and gradually stir heavy cream into mixture. Remove from stove within 2 or 3 more minutes. Garnish each serving with parsley flakes.

Serves 4 to 6

CHICKEN GUMBO

(Louisiana)

This is a soup that is made thick by the use of okra. Okra and, indeed, many of the foods we know as Southern cooking, were actually brought to the South from Western Africa by the slaves. These recipes were subsequently reproduced in plantation kitchens.

1/3 cup flour
1 teaspoon salt
freshly ground pepper
1 3-pound chicken, cut in serving pieces
bacon drippings

Spread flour on a board, and evenly sprinkle salt and pepper onto the flour. Coat pieces of chicken on all sides with this mixture. Using a skillet in which you have placed a thick layer of bacon drippings, brown chicken pieces on all side. Remove chicken and set aside.

1 10-ounce can okra
1 medium onion, chopped
1 medium green pepper, chopped
2 cups canned tomatoes and liquid
1 cup cooked shrimp
1/2 cup cooked ham, diced

1/2 teaspoon salt
2/3 teaspoon garlic powder
1/2 teaspoon hot pepper sauce
1/2 teaspoon chili powder
1 teaspoon thyme
1 bay leaf
4 cups chicken broth

Cut okra into 1/2-inch lengths and place in a Dutch oven with a little of the bacon drippings. Add onion, green pepper, tomatoes with liquid, shrimp, and ham. Season with salt, garlic powder, hot pepper sauce, chili powder, thyme, and bay leaf. Add chicken pieces, chicken broth, and sufficient water to cover all ingredients. Stir well and simmer in covered pot for 35 minutes, or until chicken is fork tender.

1-1/2 cups rice

Cook rice according to package directions. When gumbo is fully cooked, place a mound of rice in soup plates and spoon gumbo over the rice.

Serves 6 to 8

OKRA SOUP

(South Carolina)

1/2 pound bacon, fried and crumbled
1-1/2 cups canned or frozen okra, sliced
2 cups canned tomatoes, broken up, with liquid
1 green pepper, minced
1/2 pound canned or frozen lima beans
1/2 cup corn kernels
1 teaspoon salt
1 teaspoon onion powder
freshly ground pepper
2 beef bouillon cubes

In a deep saucepan, combine bacon, okra, canned tomatoes and liquid, green pepper, lima beans, and corn kernels. Add water to cover (about 1 quart). Season with salt, onion powder, and pepper. Add beef bouillon cubes. Cover and simmer over low heat for 35 minutes. Serve hot.

Serves 6 to 8

ELDERBERRY SOUP

(Northeast)

2 pints elderberries (you may have to pick them yourself)
1 quart water
1/2 cup sugar
2 teaspoons cornstarch
2 teaspoons cool water
2 tablespoons orange juice

Wash berries thoroughly in a colander or sieve under cold running water and place berries and water in a covered saucepan. Simmer over low heat until water reaches a boil. Increase heat and boil for about 6 minutes, then lower heat and simmer uncovered for 1 hour, or until berries are tender. Press the berries through a fine sieve, discarding skins and seeds. Retain juice and add sufficient water to make 4 cups of liquid. Place in a clean saucepan. Add sugar and cornstarch that has been preblended in cool water. Finally add orange juice. This may be served as a hot or cold soup. If hot, float sour cream as a garnish. If cold, floats of whipped cream are appropriate.

Serves 4 to 6

THICK LENTIL SOUP

(Washington)

Lentils are an abundant crop in the state of Washington. Although dried for use, they differ from most other dried beans in that they can be cooked in a much shorter time and never require presoaking.

1-1/2 cups dried lentils
1 meaty ham bone
4 cups beef bouillon
1 medium onion, thinly sliced
1 cup chopped celery
1-1/2 teaspoons salt
freshly ground pepper
1/2 teaspoon rosemary
1/4 teaspoon garlic powder
1 carrot, scraped and sliced
2 frankfurters, sliced

Place lentils in a deep saucepan with ham bone, and pour in beef bouillon. Add water to cover, if needed. Cover and simmer for 15 minutes. Then add onion, celery, salt, pepper, rosemary, garlic, and carrot. Allow to simmer, covered, for 45 minutes more. Add sliced frankfurters. Cover and simmer 10 more minutes.

Serves 4

OXTAIL SOUP

(Western)

cooking oil
3/4 pound oxtail, cut in pieces
6 peppercorns
2/3 teaspoon garlic powder
1 large carrot, sliced
1 cup celery, diced
1 bay leaf
1 teaspoon thyme
1 teaspoon onion powder
2 tablespoons parsley
7 cups water
1/2 cup toasted croutons

Place cooking oil in a skillet over low heat and, when the oil is hot, add the oxtail. Brown on all sides. Remove from heat and, in a large deep saucepan, combine oxtail pieces with all other ingredients except croutons. Simmer over low heat for 2-1/2 hours. Strain the broth and serve hot with croutons floating on the surface.

Serves 6

WATERCRESS SOUP

(Southern)

2 bunches watercress, washed and chopped
1/4 cup butter or margarine
1 quart water
4 large potatoes, pared and diced
2/3 cup cream
1 egg yolk, lightly beaten
1 teaspoon salt
1 teaspoon lemon juice
paprika

Add watercress and butter or margarine to water in a deep saucepan over low heat. Heat until boiling and add potatoes. Cover pot and continue simmering (lowering heat, if necessary) for 35 minutes. At this time, in a mixing bowl, combine egg yolk and cream. While stirring constantly, gradually add this to soup. Season with salt and lemon juice, and continue simmering 5 minutes more. Dust paprika over each serving.

Serves 4 to 6

PUMPKIN SOUP

(Northeast)

Pumpkins, which were introduced to the settlers by the Indians, were a familiar Colonial food.

2 cups canned pumpkin puree
2 tablespoons brown sugar
2-1/2 tablespoons butter or margarine
1 teaspoon salt
1 cup water
2 cups milk
1 cup light cream
1/2 teaspoon nutmeg

In a deep saucepan over low heat, combine pumpkin puree, brown sugar, butter, salt, and water. After about 7 minutes, gradually stir in milk, then cream. If soup is too thick, depending on consistency of canned pumpkin, add up to another cup of milk or water. Blend all ingredients well. Serve hot with nutmeg floating on top.

Serves 4 to 6

Breads

FARM BREAD

(Midwest)

1/2 cup warm water
1 envelope yeast
1-1/4 cups hot water
1-1/2 teaspoons salt
3-1/2 tablespoons honey
2 tablespoons corn oil
4-1/4 cups whole wheat flour

Preheat oven to 275 degrees. In a small bowl, dissolve the yeast in the warm water. Pour hot water into a large ovenproof bowl and add salt, honey, and corn oil. Gradually start to sift wheat flour into bowl. After sifting in about 1/4 cup of flour, add the dissolved yeast mixture.

Beat well, then continue gradually sifting in and alternately beating flour through other ingredients. When mixture is well beaten, cover bowl loosely with a cloth and place it in the oven for 15 minutes. Turn batter onto a floured board and knead with lightly floured hands. Punch the dough down from time to time, then fold until it is smooth and has an elastic consistency. Divide dough into two equal portions and turn dough in two lightly greased loaf pans. Cover each with a cloth and place in oven for 1 hour. The dough will then have risen far above pans. Remove cloth from each. Increase oven heat to 350 degrees and bake 45 minutes. Test for doneness by feeling the loaves. When they are light but firm, when the tines of a form inserted in the bread emerge cleanly, and when the crust is nicely browned, the bread is finished. Allow each loaf to cool on a rack at room temperature before slicing.

SQUAW BREAD

(Midwest, Indian)

The Plains Indians were migratory, following the buffalo herds. The Sioux, Cheyennes, Blackfoots, Dakotas, and other tribes fed on whatever wild animals their hunters brought back. Other tribes, including the Kiowa and Osage, settled for a while on the more fertile land near the great rivers and farmed corn, beans, squash, and whatever other vegetables they could. Whatever bread they ate was prepared by the women for the tribesmen.

2 cups flour
1 tablespoon baking powder
2/3 teaspoon salt
3/4 cup milk
3/4 teaspoon softened butter
cooking oil

Into a mixing bowl, sift flour, baking powder, and salt. Gradually stir in milk and softened butter. Beat mixture well. When it is firm, knead the dough on a floured board. Shape it into a round flat loaf that will fit with ease into your 10 or 12-inch skillet.

Pour the oil into the skillet to a depth of 1/4 inch. Place loaf in pan and brown over medium heat, turning bread in order to brown upper and lower sides. When both sides are sufficiently brown, remove loaf and allow to cool on wire rack. When nearly cool, cut in wedges and serve with meat, cheese, or fish spread on the bread, or eat with butter or jam.

POPOVERS

(Southern)

4 eggs, well beaten
2 cups milk, room temperature
2 cups all-purpose flour
1 teaspoon salt
1/8 teaspoon baking soda

Preheat oven to 425 degrees. In a mixing bowl, beat together beaten eggs with milk. Sift in flour, salt, and baking soda. Continue to beat, scraping sides of bowl, until all ingredients are well blended. Grease individual cups of muffin tin thoroughly. Fill each about 2/3 full of batter and bake for 20 minutes. Lower heat to 350 degrees *without opening oven door.* Continue to bake 20 minutes more. Serve hot.

Yields about 10 popovers

CRACKLIN' BREAD

(Southeast)

The early settlers made cracklin' bread with the crisp bits of pork left after lard is rendered, called by them, cracklings.

3/4 cup salt pork, finely diced
2 cups cornmeal
1-1/2 teaspoons baking powder
1/2 teaspoon baking soda
3/4 teaspoon salt
1 cup buttermilk
1 egg, well beaten
2 tablespoons salt pork cracklings

Using a skillet, without added fat, fry salt pork until it is crisply browned. Drain fat and cracklings together. Into a bowl, sift cornmeal, baking powder, baking soda, and salt. In a separate bowl, mix together the buttermilk, egg, and fatty cracklings. Grease a 7 x 11-inch baking pan and bake in 400° oven 25 to 30 minutes. A choice accompaniment to *Burgoo* or *Brunswick Stew*.

CORN BREAD

(Massachusetts)

1-1/2 cups cool (*not* cold) water
6 cups cornmeal
1/4 cup plus 1 tablespoon butter or margarine
1-1/2 teaspoons salt
1/2 cup light molasses
2 envelopes yeast
1/2 cup warm water
1-1/2 tablespoons butter or margarine, melted

In a deep saucepan over low heat, combine water, 1/2 the cornmeal, butter, salt, and molasses. Cool, with pot uncovered, until barely warm. In a small bowl, add yeast to warm water. When the yeast has dissolved and the cornmeal mixture cooled, turn dough into a greased mixing bowl and beat yeast into mixture. Beat in remaining cornmeal until dough is stiff. Flour a board and knead dough for about 8 minutes, or until dough is elastic. Place again in greased bowl. Cover with towel and keep at room temperature away from drafts. In 1-1/2 hours, dough will have doubled in bulk. Remove again to floured board. Punch dough and knead for 8 minutes. Return dough to greased bowl again for 1-1/2 hours to redouble in bulk. Preheat oven to 375 degrees. Turn dough into two loaf pans and paint melted butter across top with pastry brush. Bake 45 to 55 minutes, or until loaves are brown and emit a hollow sound when tapped. Allow to cool at room temperature on wire rack. When completely cool, wrap in plastic wrap. To serve slice as any bread.

SHORT'NIN' BREAD

(Southern)

Actually, they are cookies—delicious enough to have been immortalized in song. Mammy baked them, her li'l baby sang of them, and anyone who tastes them wants more.

2 cups all-purpose flour
1/2 cup granulated (or light) brown sugar
1/2 pound softened butter

Into a mixing bowl, sift flour and add sugar and softened butter gradually, working until mixture is fully smooth. Wrap plastic wrap loosely about dough and refrigerate 1/2 hour.

Flour a board and roll dough to 1/2-inch thickness. Cut into small squares or oblongs and place on cookie sheet. Bake in 325° oven for 20 to 25 minutes, removing when cookies are lightly browned.

Makes about 2 dozen cookies

BUTTERMILK SODA BISCUITS

(Eastern)

1 tablespoon butter or margarine
1-1/4 cups all-purpose flour
3/4 tablespoon baking powder
1/3 teaspoon salt
3 tablespoons butter, melted
1/2 cup plus 1 tablespoon buttermilk

Preheat oven to 475 degrees. Grease baking sheet with 1 tablespoon butter. In a mixing bowl, sift flour with baking powder and salt. Punch a well in the mixture and into this pour melted butter and buttermilk. Beat very well for at least 4 minutes, but do not overbeat, as this will ensure having biscuits turn out light. Roll dough on floured board to a thickness of 1/2 inch. Using the rim of a glass or a biscuit cutter, divide the batter into 2-inch rounds. Make new rounds by rolling scraps together. Place rounds on baking sheet without touching. Bake for about 12 minutes, when biscuits will be lightly browned. Serve hot with butter or jam.

Yields about 1 dozen biscuits

SPOON BREAD

(Southeast)

This is so called because it is porridgelike and is eaten with a spoon. It is an adaptation of an Indian recipe made of cornmeal.

1 cup cornmeal
1 teaspoon sugar
1/2 teaspoon salt
4 tablespoons butter or margarine
1-1/2 cups hot milk
3 eggs

Grease a 1-quart casserole. In a mixing bowl, combine cornmeal, sugar, salt, and butter or margarine. Mix well and add hot milk, mixing thoroughly. Beat eggs well and stir into mixture. Turn mixture into casserole and bake 30 to 35 minutes in a 375° oven. Serve hot with a dab of butter atop each portion.

Serves 4 to 6

Meats

ROAST BEEF AND YORKSHIRE PUDDING

(Eastern)

Although English in origin, this was a favored meal among English colonists—later United States citizens. During the Revolution, beef was scarce.

rib roast (allow 3 servings to the pound)
8 small onions
8 medium potatoes, cut in thirds
1 teaspoon salt
freshly ground pepper

Preheat oven to 500 degrees. Place thawed beef on a rack within a pan and arrange onions and potatoes around the beef. Sprinkle salt on meat and rub on pepper. Roast for 10 minutes, then lower heat to 325 degrees. Allow 18 to 20 minutes roasting time to the pound for rare; 20 to 22 minutes for medium-done; 23 to 27 minutes for well-done. (Preferably use a meat thermometer.)

YORKSHIRE PUDDING

1 cup all-purpose flour
1/2 teaspoon salt
1 cup milk
2 eggs
beef pan drippings

Preheat oven to 425 degrees and heat 9 x 12-inch pan in oven. Sift flour and salt into bowl. Pour milk in at once and beat hard until well blended. Break in eggs and continue beating. Remove pan from oven and pour in beef drippings, turning pan to cover lower surface. Turn batter into pan and bake 15 minutes. Lower heat to 350 degrees and continue baking 15 minutes longer, or until pudding is puffed and brown.

Serves 6

YANKEE POT ROAST I

(Northeast)

1 tablespoon corn oil
4 pounds bottom or top round beef roast
1 teaspoon salt
freshly ground pepper
1 large onion, coarsely chopped
1 tablespoon chopped parsley
1 large carrot, scraped and chopped
2 tablespoons flour

Spread a light layer of oil across the bottom of a Dutch oven. Place roast in pot over low heat, turning beef until browned on all sides. When properly browned, add water to about 1/2 of the pot capacity. Season meat with salt and pepper, and add onion, parsley, and carrot. Continue to cook slowly with the pot covered for 2-1/2 hours. At that time check meat with fork for doneness and, if not sufficiently tender, continue cooking for 15 minutes longer and repeat fork test. When meat is tender, place in a large bowl. Strain gravy to free it of all ingredients. Pour strained gravy over meat and refrigerate, covering with plastic wrap. Any fat in the gravy will congeal. Remove this. Pour the remaining gravy into Dutch oven over low heat. Gradually stir in flour a little at a time, so that gravy will not become lumpy. Stir constantly. When gravy has thickened, add the meat and heat covered for about 12 minutes, until meat is hot.

Serves 6 to 8

YANKEE POT ROAST II

(Northeast)

Another method of cooking pot roast is to bake it. The result is every bit as traditional.

1 tablespoon corn oil
4 pounds bottom or top round beef roast
1 large onion, coarsely chopped
1 teaspoon salt
freshly ground pepper
1 tablespoon Worcestershire sauce
2 tablespoons flour

Preheat oven to 425 degrees. Using a heavy skillet over low heat, quickly brown meat on all sides, removing before meat can stick to skillet. Immediately place meat on a wire rack in roasting pan (with cover). Sprinkle onion, salt, and pepper over meat and rub in Worcestershire sauce. Add water to fill pan

1/3 to brim. Cover pan and bake 3-1/2 hours. At that time reduce heat to 350 degrees and continue baking 1-1/2 hours. Meat should then be fork tender. Allow to cool at room temperature until fat somewhat congeals. Skim fat and thicken gravy by pouring portion of gravy into a small saucepan over low heat. Gradually add flour, stirring constantly so that flour will not be lumpy. Return thickened gravy to pan and mix. Return covered roasting pot to oven for 10 minutes to heat meat and gravy.

Serves 6 to 8

YANKEE POT ROAST III

(New England)

4 pounds bottom or top round beef roast
3/4 teaspoon salt
freshly ground pepper
4 tablespoons butter or margarine
1 large onion, coarsely chopped
2 cups beef bouillon
1 bay leaf
sprinkling of black peppercorns (about 8)
1 tablespoon parsley flakes
4 medium carrots, scraped, cut in 1-inch lengths
4 medium potatoes, peeled, cut up
1 tablespoon flour

Season meat with salt and pepper. In a Dutch oven, melt butter or margarine over low flame and brown meat on all sides. Remove beef and sauté onion. Return meat to pot. Add beef bouillon and water to bring liquid level to 1/2 of the pot. Add bay leaf, black peppercorns, and parsley flakes. Cover pot and simmer for about 2-1/2 hours. Add carrots and potatoes and continue simmering, covered, for 1/2 hour more. Test meat with a fork. If tender, remove pot roast and vegetables to a heated platter. Discard bay leaf. Continue cooking liquid on a somewhat higher flame. When liquid is reduced in quantity, stir in flour, making sure that no lumps of flour remain.

Slice meat and serve with vegetables. Serve the gravy in a boat or bowl, for optional use by diners.

Serves 4 to 6

STEAK DIANE

(New York City)

This recipe is one that has built the fame of New York City fine restaurants.

1/2 cup butter or margarine
2-1/2 pounds round steak, 1/4-inch thick, cut into 5 portions
1 small onion, chopped
2 tablespoons chili sauce
1 tablespoon Worcestershire sauce
1 teaspoon prepared mustard
1 teaspoon salt
freshly ground pepper
1/3 cup brandy
parsley sprigs

In a skillet, melt butter over low heat. Add individual steaks and cook for 2 minutes on each side. Remove steaks to a platter. Combine all other ingredients, with the exception of brandy and parsley, and heat in skillet over low heat for 3 minutes. Return steaks to skillet, spooning sauce over each. Cook 1 minute more on each side. Pour brandy over all. Remove skillet from stove and set brandy aflame. Garnish with parsley sprigs and serve.

Serves 5

PAN-FRIED PORTERHOUSE STEAK

(New York City)

3-1/2 pounds porterhouse steak, (1-1/2 inches thick)
1 teaspoon salt
1/2 teaspoon garlic powder
2 onions, sliced and separated into thin rings
1 cup fresh mushrooms, sliced

Place steak in heated pan. Fat is not required, as fat from the meat is sufficient. Season meat with salt and garlic powder. Place onion rings and mushrooms around the steak in the pan. Turn heat high and fry no more than 6 minutes on each side. Steak so prepared should be served raw inside. Top steak with mushrooms and onion. Serve with baked potato and salad.

Serves 3 or 4

FLANK STEAK

(Midwest, Shaker)

The Shakers were a farming people, and their food reflects their love of the land. All of the ingredients of their recipes were obtained from within their own communes. Unlike the Pennsylvania Dutch, who were usually of Germanic birth or origin and who didn't share a common religion, the Shakers migrated from the Manchester, England area. They originally settled in a town near Albany, New York, but the sect spread widely as a result of the preaching of its founder, Mother Ann Lee, who attempted to convert others to her way of life.

Shakers established themselves throughout New England and later throughout Ohio, Indiana, and Kentucky. Since all sex was forbidden, they produced no offspring, and their numbers had to be increased by conversion. Shaker communities still exist, but there are not many members.

It was in the production of food that the Shakers excelled. They believed in eating "hearty" and "clearing out our plates." Their food was simple and well seasoned with herbs, the chief among which was sage.

1/4 pound butter or margarine
2-1/2 pounds flank steak
1 teaspoon salt
freshly ground pepper
1 cup fresh mushrooms, sliced
2 medium onions, chopped
2 carrots, scraped and sliced
2 tablespoons parsley flakes

In a deep skillet, melt butter or margarine over low heat. Place steak in pan and season with salt and pepper. Add mushrooms, onions, carrots, and parsley flakes. Cover and simmer 1-3/4 hours, or until steak is tender. Check occasionally after 1/2 hour to be certain that there are sufficient pan juices to keep steak from sticking to pan or burning. Add a little water if needed. Mash vegetables with a spoon and serve over the meat with juices as a sauce.

Serves 4 to 6

OVEN BARBECUED SPARE RIBS

(Southwest)

In the latter 1800s political barbecues took favor as a pretelevision way of swaying voters. Then, whole sides of beef and entire pigs were spitted above flames. Today, the quantity is modified for patio or terrace dining, or it can be a barbecue in your oven.

2 racks of spareribs, cut into eating-size pieces
1-1/2 teaspoons salt
freshly ground pepper

Preheat oven to 350 degrees. Sprinkle salt and pepper over spareribs and arrange on a rack set in roasting pan. Set aside while you prepare Barbecue Sauce.

BARBECUE SAUCE

1-1/2 cups tomato juice
1/2 cup vinegar
1 medium onion, minced
3/4 teaspoon garlic powder
1/4 cup tomato ketchup
1/4 cup Worcestershire sauce
1/3 teaspoon mustard powder
3/4 teaspoon salt
freshly ground pepper
1/4 cup brown sugar

In a large bowl, blend all ingredients well and spoon some of the sauce over the spare-ribs. Place spareribs in over 30 minutes. Turn occasionally and baste with sauce, continuing to do so all during roasting. Increase heat after 1/2 hour to 425 degrees, and continue roasting 25 minutes more, when ribs should be nicely browned. Extra sauce may be served with spareribs.

Serves 6

SMITHFIELD COUNTRY HAM

(Virginia)

It was necessary to preserve meats over long periods of time without refrigeration. In Virginia (as in neighboring states), it was the custom to hang raw hams cut from porkers that had been fed corn, peanuts, acorns, some fallen fruit, and likely kettle slop and bits of gristle and other table scraps. In the South, hams were dry-cured. Because salt is a preservative, they were salted. Available spices and herbs were also rubbed into the flesh. Then the hams were hung up in a smokehouse (often a lean-to type of small shack) and exposed to smoke given off by fragrant woods for several days. After this, the hams were allowed to cool and were then wrapped in a burlap-type cloth and buried in the cool ashes —for several months or years. Upon use, the brine, which had formed a crust on the ham, had to be scraped off so that all of the mold was removed before preparation.

1 ham (weighed)
1 quart apple cider vinegar
1/2 cup honey
3/4 cup brown sugar
freshly ground pepper
1/8 teaspoon ground ginger
1/4 teaspoon mustard powder

In a Dutch oven over low heat, place ham in vinegar and add sufficient water to cover. Immediately stir in honey and brown sugar, and season with pepper, ginger, and mustard powder. Simmer the ham for 25 minutes per pound. When sufficiently cooked according to weight of ham, remove to a roasting pan and preset oven to 475 degrees.

1 cup cornmeal
1/2 cup brown sugar
1/4 cup apple cider vinegar

Spread cornmeal on a board and roll the ham in it. In a small bowl, combine brown sugar and vinegar, and baste the ham with this. Roast ham for 10 minutes, then turn down oven heat to 425 degrees. If possible, use a ham thermometer, as it is most important that ham be thoroughly done when eaten. If one is not available, again determine cooking time according to poundage. Allow about 22 minutes to the pound. Allow to cool somewhat before carving in very thin slices.

SPARERIBS

(Southwest)

4 pounds spareribs
1/2 cup lemon juice
2 tabelspoons Worcestershire sauce
1/2 cup brown sugar
1 teaspoon onion powder
1/2 teaspoon garlic powder
1 teaspoon salt
freshly ground pepper

Preheat oven to 475 degrees. Place spareribs on a rack in a baking pan. Spoon lemon juice and Worcestershire sauce over spareribs and sprinkle on brown sugar, onion powder, garlic powder, salt, and pepper. Bake 10 minutes, then reduce heat to 350 degrees and continue baking for an additional 1 hour 40 minutes, or until fork tender.

Serves 4 to 6

HICKORY SMOKED HAM

(Tennessee)

Boiling

A country-raised, sugar-cured, hickory-smoked ham is worth the additional expense and, in the long run, is not really much more expensive. It will deliciously feed a large group at a party or will keep in the freezer to be used as needed. If the ham is extremely large, it will require halving it and cooking it in two large pots, eating what you can, and, again, freezing the remainder.

Accurately weigh the ham so that cooking time can be calculated. Thoroughly scrub down the ham before cooking since it has been hanging nigh onto a year in the farmer's smokehouse. Soak it in the cooking pot for 1/2 hour. Cover ham with water, cover the pot, and cook over moderate heat until the water begins to boil. Lower heat and simmer for about 25 minutes to the pound.

When done, remove the ham from the pot. Cut off the outer skin and most of the fat layer, but leave enough to score in a diamond pattern, and then insert a clove in each diamong.

Note: The cooking liquid is useful in other cookery.

Place ham, scored side up, on a rack in a shallow roasting pan.

1 cup brown sugar
3 tablespoons honey
1/2 cup apple cider
1/4 teaspoon mustard powder
1/8 teaspoon ginger
3 tablespoons orange juice

In a small bowl, mix all ingredients well. After ham is arranged on rack set in roasting pan, ladle the sauce over the ham.

Bake in 325 degree oven, basting occasionally, allowing 10 minutes to the pound.

Serve hot or cold, sliced.

The number of persons served is determined by size of ham. Allow approximately 3/4 pound per person.

BROILED LIVER

(Chicago)

"They say such things and do such things" in Chicago, but one of the City's best culinary achievements is this simple recipe for a hearty meat.

2 pounds liver (beef, or calf), sliced 1-inch thick
1/2 teaspoon salt
freshly ground pepper

Cut steaks into 4 portions and place directly on broiler pan. Season with 1/2 the salt and pepper. Broil 5 minutes, then turn meat, season with remaining salt and pepper, and broil underside for 4 minutes more. Test for doneness by inserting the tip of a very sharp knife. If blood exudes from cut, continue broiling 1 minute more, then recheck, inserting knife in a different portion of the steak. Do not allow to overcook, as liver has a tendency to toughen quickly. Optionally, sprinkle fried bacon crumbs or half-fried onion rings over liver.

Serves 4

MARINATED PORK LOIN

(Alabama)

This meat is cooked best in this state, where they not only raise porkers but know how to deliciously bring them to table.

4-pound pork loin

MARINADE

1-1/2 cups wine vinegar
2 cloves garlic, crushed
1 medium onion, minced
1 medium carrot, scraped and sliced
10 peppercorns
1 bay leaf
1 teaspoon thyme
1/8 teaspoon powdered mustard

Place meat in a deep bowl containing all of the marinade ingredients. Spoon some of the marinade over the pork loin. Cover the bowl with plastic wrap, sealing all edges, and refrigerate. After 3 hours, turn the meat and again spoon marinade over it. Continue turning and basting meat for at least 8 hours, but preferably for 24 hours. Refrigerate for entire period. Preheat oven to 375 degrees. Lift pork loin from marinade, reserving marinade for basting during roasting. Place meat on a rack in a roasting pan. After 10 minutes, reduce heat to 325 degrees. Preferably use a meat thermometer. Otherwise allow a full 40 minutes to the pound (no less). Baste frequently with remaining marinade. Allow meat to remain in oven with door open while you ready the dinner for serving. A green vegetable, potato, and a relish make excellent accompaniment.

Serves 6

PORK WITH SAUERKRAUT AND DUMPLINGS

(Pennsylvania Dutch)

3 pounds pork loin or shoulder
3 pounds sauerkraut
1 teaspoon salt
freshly ground pepper

Place pork in a deep, heavy saucepan, with enough water to cover pork. Simmer 2-1/2 hours, or until pork is fork tender. Add sauerkraut, salt, and pepper. Uncover saucepan and cook 3/4 hour longer.

DUMPLINGS

3/4 cup all-purpose flour
1/2 teaspoon baking powder
1/4 teaspoon salt
2 eggs, beaten
1/4 cup milk

Sift flour, baking powder, and salt into mixing bowl. Add beaten egg, stirring well, and slowly add milk. Use only enough milk to make a stiff batter—you may not need the entire 1/4 cupful. When the batter is well mixed, drop by tablespoonfuls onto the cooking sauerkraut. Be careful not to let the dough drop into the liquid. Once the dumplings are cooking on the bed of sauerkraut, cover the saucepan and lower the heat. Do not peek under cover for at least 25 minutes, so that the dumplings can steam.

Serves 6 to 8

PORK SCRAPPLE

(Maryland and Pennsylvania)

The Pennsylvania Dutch people were never "Dutch" at all. The word is taken from *Deutsch*, which means German. These people were impelled by religious persecution to settle in Maryland and Pennsylvania before Revolutionary times. Their food is distinctive and delicious.

2 cups lean pork, minced
1/4 pound pork liver, minced
2 teaspoons salt
1 small onion, finely chopped
1 cup cornmeal
1 cup cold water
1/8 teaspoon powdered cloves
1 teaspoon marjoram
1 teaspoon sage
freshly ground pepper
oil for frying

Place pork and liver in a saucepan half-filled with water and simmer for 1 hour over moderate heat, reducing heat when water comes to a boil. Season with salt. In a bowl, combine onion and cornmeal with cold water and season with cloves, marjoram, sage, and pepper. Add this mixture to cooking pork and stir well until mixture thickens somewhat. Add a bit more cornmeal, if required, but always do so sparingly. When mixture has thickened sufficiently, remove from heat and spoon into a loaf pan. Refrigerate overnight, or at least for 6 to 7 hours. If a crust is not desired, cover with plastic wrap, sealing all edges. Cut in 1/2-inch slices and brown in a skillet before use, greasing skillet with a scant amount of oil. Serve hot.

Serves 6

PORK SAUSAGE

(Milwaukee)

In this era of delicatessens and packages of processed sausages, it may seem quaint to suggest that sausage be made at home. It was in years gone by and, if you will take the time, both pure ingredients and an old-time taste treat will be yours. Sausage casings may be purchased in many butcher shops. If none are readily available, you may substitute plastic wrap.

1-1/2 pounds cooked pork, ground (both fat and meat)
1 clove garlic, minced
1 teaspoon thyme
1 teaspoon salt
freshly ground pepper
1 medium onion, minced
1/2 teaspoon sage

In a mixing bowl, combine ground pork with garlic, thyme, salt, pepper, onion, and sage and blend thoroughly. Stuff the sausage casing full, or shape the mixture into a long roll and wrap tightly in plastic wrap, allowing no air spaces. Refrigerate and serve cold and sliced, or fry slices and serve with eggs and German fried (pan-fried) potatoes.

Serves 4 to 6

ROAST SHOULDER OF VEAL

(New Jersey)

1 3-pound rolled shoulder of veal
2 cloves garlic, crushed
3 tablespoons butter or margarine
1 teaspoon salt
freshly ground pepper
1 tablespoon paprika
1-1/2 teaspoons rosemary
1 onion, minced
1-1/4 cups tomato juice

Preheat oven to 375 degrees. Using the tip of a kitchen knife, make incisions 1/2-inch deep across the top of the roast. In a small bowl, combine garlic, butter, salt, pepper, paprika, and rosemary. Press this mixture into the slits and, with your hands, spread any remainder across the veal. Place veal on a rack in a roasting pan. Pour tomato juice over meat and sprinkle onion pieces over all. If possible, use a meat thermometer. Roast 1-3/4 hours, basting meat several times during roasting. If gravy is desired, remove meat to a warm plate and add 1-1/2 teaspoons flour to pan juices. Heat this, stirring constantly.

Serves 5 or 6

CONEY WIENER

(Brooklyn)

Off the wide Atlantic beaches, Coney Island, in New York City's famed borough of Brooklyn, became well known, at the turn of the nineteenth century, as a nearly fashionable resort. In later years, its exclusiveness paled, but not the fun to be had there in the amusement parks with ferris wheels, loop-the-loops, otherwise known as scenic railways, merry-go-rounds, and other participating amusements. Of equal importance is the hot dog, or wiener. Here is a recipe for it.

1 pound wieners (about 6)
1 medium onion, coarsely chopped
1 tablespoon oil
2 tablespoons Worcestershire sauce
2 tablespoons tomato catsup
1 teaspoon prepared mustard
1/2 cup water

Cut wieners in half lengthwise and set aside. Brown onion in oil in a skillet over low heat. As soon as the onion turns golden (about 7 minutes), add wieners and spoon Worcestershire sauce, tomato catsup, and mustard over each equally. Add water, cover skillet, and allow to simmer for 15 minutes. Remove cover and continue cooking for 7 minutes more.

Serves 6

REUBEN SANDWICH

(New York City)

This is the sandwich (really a meal) that a famous eatery devised and gave its name to.

8 slices pumpernickel bread
1 tablespoon butter or margarine
3/4 pound lean corned beef, thinly sliced
3/4 pound Swiss cheese, thinly sliced
1-1/4 cups sauerkraut (drain liquid)
mustard

Each sandwich requires 2 slices of bread. Lightly butter 4 of these slices. These buttered sides are to be placed on the grill to keep the sandwiches from sticking to it. Divide corned beef in four portions, and place some on the dry side of the bread just buttered. Place Swiss cheese slices and a layer of sauerkraut on top of the meat. Top with unbuttered slice of bread. Put a heavy plate over each sandwich and place on a hot grill, or in a heated skillet, or in a heated metal baking pan set over the stove burners. Heat for about 7 to 8 minutes, or until cheese has just become runny. Serve with mustard for optional use.

Serves 4

ROAST MOOSE

(Alaska)

This hulking, flat-antlered animal is the largest member of the deer family. It does not have the grace or beauty of a deer, but is of enormous size, with a long snout and muzzle. Alaska is home to the largest of the moose, often weighing well over 1,700 pounds.

Its meat is not to be found in butcher shops and, although many Alaskans favor moose venison, they must make their own kill or share a moose killed by a friend. The cuts correspond to the familiar ones for beef.

1 5 or 6 pound moose rib roast
1 teaspoon garlic powder
1-1/2 teaspoons salt
freshly ground pepper
8 strips bacon

Preheat oven to 350 degrees. Rub garlic, salt, and pepper into the meat. With toothpicks, secure bacon strips to meat. Place meat on a rack in a roasting pan and roast, allowing 30 minutes to the pound. Insert an oven thermometer into the meat. When this registers 140 degrees, the meat is rare; 150 degrees, medium-done; 160 degrees, well-done.

Serves 6 to 8

BROILED CARIBOU STEAK

(Alaska)

The caribou is a large, palmate-antlered deer, related to the reindeer. Its meat is enjoyed by native Alaskans and, if the animal is a young one, a caribou steak is quite delicious. Its cuts are similar to those of beef or lamb.

4 slices lean caribou steak, 1 inch or more thick
1 cup cooking oil
3/4 cup vinegar
1 teaspoon salt
freshly ground pepper
1 clove garlic, minced
1 teaspoon onion powder
4 strips bacon

Place steaks in a deep pan or dish, pour oil and vinegar over them, and allow to marinate at room temperature for 1-1/2 hours.

Remove steaks to a greased baking pan, season with salt and pepper, and sprinkle with garlic pieces and onion powder. Place a strip of bacon across each steak and broil 3 inches from flame for about 8 to 10 minutes on each side for rare; 10 to 12 minutes for medium; and 13 to 15 minutes for well done.

Serves 4

BROILED REINDEER STEAK

(Alaska)

The reindeer is another deer and, as such, reindeer venison is a part of many an Alaskan's diet.

4 reindeer steaks, 3/4 to 1 inch thick
3/4 teaspoon salt
freshly ground pepper
3/4 teaspoon onion powder
2 tablespoons butter

Apply salt, pepper, and onion powder to steaks. Dot the steaks with butter and place on a broiling rack about 3 inches from flame. Allow about 3 minutes on each side for rare steak, 4 to 5 minutes for medium, and about 6-1/2 minutes for well-done (which last I do not recommend, as meat might get leathery).

Serve with baked potatoes and salad.

Serves 4

SOUTH SEAS LAMB CHOPS

(Hawaii)

1/2 cup corn oil
1 teaspoon salt
freshly ground pepper
2 tablespoons soy sauce
1/4 cup orange juice
1/4 cup vinegar
1-1/2 cups fresh pineapple, cut in cubes
6 lamb chops (shoulder or steaks from leg), cut 1-inch thick

Combine all ingredients in a baking pan and blend thoroughly. Marinate lamb chops in a mixture for 3/4 hour. Using same pan, place chops under broiler heat. Broil top side for 10 minutes, then turn and broil underside for 8 minutes more.

Serves 6

FRUITED VEAL CHOPS

(California)

2 tablespoons flour
1 teaspoon salt
freshly ground pepper
4 veal chops (rib or loin), cut 1-inch thick
1 tablespoon oil
4 canned pear halves, with liquid
8 canned apricot halves, with liquid
1/2 teaspoon onion powder
1-1/2 tablespoons Worcestershire sauce

In a wide bowl, combine flour, salt, and pepper and dip chops in this to season. Heat oil in a skillet over low heat and, before it can smoke, add veal chops. Brown on both sides (about 4 minutes on each side). Add pear and apricot halves, with juices. Season with onion powder and blend Worcestershire sauce with fruit liquid. Spoon liquid over chops and cover skillet. Continue simmering over low heat for 35 minutes. Remove cover and continue to simmer 10 minutes more.

Serves 4

CREOLE PORK CHOPS

(Southern)

1 tablespoon oil
4 pork chops (if small, double quantity)
1 small onion, coarsely chopped
2 cups tomato sauce
2 tablespoons brown sugar
1 teaspoon salt
freshly ground pepper
1/4 teaspoon thyme
1 cup uncooked rice
1-1/4 cup water

Heat oil in a skillet over low heat. Place pork chops, then onion, in pan and pour tomato sauce over all. Add brown sugar, salt, pepper, and thyme. Stir in uncooked rice and add water, stirring well. Cover skillet and simmer, keeping heat low, 35 minutes or until chops are thoroughly cooked and rice done.

Serves 4

COWBOY LAMB

(Southwest)

1 6-pound leg of lamb
1 teaspoon salt
freshly ground pepper
1 teaspoon garlic powder
1 teaspoon rosemary

Season lamb with salt, pepper, garlic powder, and rosemary. If possible, cook this out-of-doors on an electrically operated spit. Place the lamb on the spit over coals. However, if you cook in your kitchen, preheat the oven to 375 degrees and place lamb on a rack in a roasting pan. Roast 1 hour and 45 minutes, when lamb should be nearly done. It is advisable to use a meat thermometer. Baste with pan juices and continue roasting for 35 minutes more. Lamb will be well done. (For rotisserie roasting, timing should be about the same.)

Serves 6 or 7

BOILED BEEF

(Southeast)

3-1/2 pound brisket of beef (your choice of cut)
2 onions, cut into quarters
2 carrots, scraped and cut into 1-inch lengths
1 white turnip, cut into eighths
1 teaspoon salt
8 peppercorns
1 bay leaf
4 medium potatoes, cut into thirds
1 small head cabbage, cut into wedges

In a Dutch oven, place the meat, onions, carrots, and turnip in sufficient water to cover meat. Over moderate heat, bring liquid to a boil, then lower heat. Salt the meat, and add peppercorns, bay leaf, and potatoes. Keeping heat low, simmer 2-1/4 hours, or until meat is fork tender. During last 1/2 hour of cooking, add cabbage. Slice meat and serve with vegetables from pot.

Serves 4 to 6

(One-Pot Meals)

Some of our earliest and most flavorsome recipes were stews—combinations of available ingredients that offer gourmet flavors and aromas.

RAILROAD STATION OYSTER STEW

(New York City)

Some say it's more soup than stew, but we'll abide by its name.

In bygone days, many a traveler in Grand Central Station turned the disadvantage of a train wait into the enjoyment of an oyster stew in the famous lower level restaurant, thereby improving the state of both nerves and stomach.

2-1/2 tablespoons butter
1 teaspoon celery salt
1 teaspoon onion powder
1 quart cleaned oysters, with liquid
3 cups milk
1 cup light cream
freshly ground pepper
1/8 teaspoon paprika
1-1/2 tablespoons chopped parsley
oyster crackers

Place butter, celery salt, and onion powder in a deep saucepan and melt butter over low heat. Add oyster liquid and oysters. Simmer, uncovered, until oysters begin curling at the edges. Gradually stir in milk and light cream, and season with pepper. Stir constantly with slow measure over low heat. Remove from stove as soon as milk and cream are heated. Serve in bowls and garnish each portion with a sprinkling of paprika and chopped parsley. Small hexagonal oyster crackers should be served with the stew.

Serves 6

INDIAN BEAN STEW

(Colorado)

Pinto beans are spotted and are a staple in the Southwest. Should you be unable to obtain them in another region of the United States, substitute red kidney beans.

1 pound dried pinto beans
1 lamb shank, cracked
1 large onion, chopped
1 clove garlic, pressed
1 bay leaf
(about 10) peppercorns
1 teaspoon salt
6 slices bacon, cut in 1-1/2 inch pieces
2 tablespoons vinegar
1/4 cup brown sugar
1 cup canned tomatoes, (with liquid)

Wash beans and place them in deep, heavy saucepan with lamb shank. Add water until saucepan is half full. Add lamb, cover, and simmer for 4 hours, or until beans are tender and meat falls from bone. Remove bone and discard, and cut lamb into bite-sized pieces. Add onion, garlic, bay leaf, peppercorns, salt, bacon, vinegar, brown sugar, and tomatoes, having first reduced the liquid in a pot, if excessive. Cover and simmer for 1 additional hour. Drain excess liquid, if any, when cooking is done.

Serves 6 to 8

BRUNSWICK STEW

(Virginia)

Both North Carolina and Virginia have a Brunswick county, and each claims this recipe.

1 3-pound chicken, cut into serving pieces
2 teaspoons salt
freshly ground pepper
1 bay leaf
1 16-ounce can tomatoes
1 16-ounce can lima beans
1 10-ounce package frozen okra
1 10-ounce can corn kernels
1 large onion, chopped
1/2 teaspoon thyme
1/2 teaspoon garlic powder
1 teaspoon Tabasco sauce
3-1/2 tablespoons butter
1/3 cup flour

Place chicken pieces, including neck, liver, and heart, in deep saucepan with water to cover. Season with salt and pepper, and add bay leaf. Cook over moderate heat until mixture just begins to boil. Lower heat and skim scum from surface as needed. Simmer, covered, for 50 minutes, then add tomatoes, lima beans, okra, corn, and onion. Season with thyme, garlic powder, and Tabasco sauce. Again cover and simmer for 45 minutes longer.

In a saucepan, melt butter over low heat and gradually stir in flour. When flour is dissolved, continue simmering, uncovered, for 10 minutes. Slowly add mixture to the stew while stirring constantly. Continue heating and stirring until stew thickens.

Serves 6 to 8

SON OF A BITCH STEW

(Arizona)

This dish has more names than a field has gopher holes, but why go into describing the less picturesque ones? However, it should be mentioned that another telling name for this recipe is mother-in-law stew. This recipe is a cattleman's mainstay on the ranches. Traditionally, all of the meat ingredients are from a newly butchered calf.

Some explanation may be needed as to what the first ingredient, marrow gut, is. All cud-chewing animals have two stomachs, and marrow gut is the name given the tube connecting the stomachs. The marrow gut is wholly edible only if the animal has not yet been weaned from a milk diet. The marrow gut used has partially digested milk still encased in its sheath, and the milk resembles a marrowlike substance. If you cannot obtain calf marrow gut, you should be able to buy veal marrow gut.

3 feet of marrow gut
1-1/2 pounds sweetbreads
1/2 pound liver
1-1/4 pounds lean rib steak
1 pound calves tongue (small)
flour
1-1/2 teaspoons salt
freshly ground pepper
beef fat
1/2 pound brains
1 teaspoon sage
1 clove garlic
1 large onion, chopped
1 tablespoon sugar

Wash all meat and wipe. Cut marrow gut, sweetbreads, liver, steak, and tongue into bite-sized pieces. Spread flour on a board and sprinkle salt and pepper over the flour. Roll cut-up meat in flour mixture.

Melt beef fat in a Dutch oven over low heat and add all meat except brains. Cover with water and simmer for 4-1/2 hours. Should the water cook down, add more during cooking.

Soak the brains for 3 hours in cold water in a deep bowl. Then remove the membrane and cut the brains into bite-sized pieces. Melt a bit more beef fat in a skillet and brown the brains on all sides. After the stew has cooked for 4-1/2 hours, add the sauteed brains, sage, garlic, onion, and sugar. Simmer for at least 1 hour more, or until marrow gut is fork tender, for a total stewing time of about 5-1/2 hours.

Serves 10 to 16 people

GOOP

(Montana)

The combination of chicken, veal, and other ingredients is a tempting one, despite the unappetizing name. Goop is a popular buffet dish.

2 tablespoons butter or margarine
1 3-1/2 pound chicken, cut into serving pieces
1/2 pound veal
1 teaspoon salt
freshly ground pepper
2 tablespoons butter or margarine (separate from above)
1 medium onion, chopped
1 small green pepper, chopped
1/2 pound mushrooms, sliced
1 cup pitted black olives
1 8-ounce package noodles
1-1/2 cups grated Cheddar cheese

Melt butter in a Dutch oven over a slow flame. Add chicken and brown on all sides. Add warm water to cover and veal. Season with salt and pepper, cover, and simmer for 2 hours. When veal is fork tender, remove chicken and veal to cutting board. Skin and bone chicken and cut veal into bite-sized pieces.

Melt butter in a skillet over low heat and add onion, green pepper, mushrooms, and olives.

Cook noodles in a deep pot, according to package instructions. When the noodles are tender, drain and add grated cheese. Stir well and add chicken, veal, and skillet mixture, blending all ingredients well.

Serves 6 to 8

BURGOO

(Kentucky)

Originally prepared on Derby Day, Kentuckians enjoy this hearty dish too much to keep it as a once-a-year recipe.

1 pound boneless lean beef
1/2 pound boneless shoulder of lamb
1 pound chicken parts
1 bay leaf
1 tablespoon parsley, minced
1 teaspoon salt
1/8 teaspoon pepper

Clean beef, lamb, and chicken, place in a Dutch oven, and cover with water. Add bay leaf, parsley, salt, and pepper, cover pot, and cook over moderate heat until boiling. Reduce heat and skim, as required. Simmer 2-1/4 hours.

2/3 cup lima beans
2 medium potatoes, pared and cut into bite-sized pieces
1 large onion, cut in eighths
2 carrots, scraped and cut in 1-inch lengths
2/3 cup canned okra
1/2 teaspoon garlic powder

Add all vegetables to Burgoo pot and, stirring occasionally, simmer over lowered heat for 45 minutes more, or until all ingredients are tender. Divide beef and lamb into portions and serve in soup plates with a piece of chicken, vegetables, and broth. Accompany with crusty bread.

Serves 6 to 8

CHILI CON CARNE

(Southwest)

There is a strong Mexican influence in much of the cooking of the Southwest border states. This influence originated when Mexican cooks were employed on the ranches. *Chili con carne* is familiar to most of us as beans with seasonings and beef, although the Mexicans prefer lamb or mutton. However, even in the Southwest beef is more greatly enjoyed in this dish, so this recipe calls for beef.

2 cups dried pinto or kidney beans
3 tablespoons butter or bacon drippings
2 medium onions, coarsely chopped
2 cloves garlic, minced
3 tablespoons chili powder
1 teaspoon salt
2 pounds lean ground beef
1 tablespoon cumin
2/3 teaspoon coriander
1/2 teaspoon oregano
1-1/4 teaspoons salt
freshly ground pepper
2 cups canned tomatoes, drained
3 tablespoons flour
3 tablespoons cold water

Place beans in a deep saucepan. Cover with cold water and allow to stand overnight. Replace water and simmer for about 1-1/2 hours, until tender. The water should be nearly evaporated when the beans are fully cooked.

In a Dutch oven, melt butter or bacon drippings. Add onions, garlic, chili powder, salt, and the meat. Add cumin, coriander, oregano, salt, and pepper. Mix all ingredients thoroughly. Add sufficient water to cover. Simmer 1-1/4 hours with cover on. Stir tomatoes through, breaking them up as you work.

In a small bowl, mix flour and water and stir into the chili. Add drained cooked pinto beans and mix well. Serve in bowls with salted soda crackers.

Serves 6 to 8

BOILED DINNER

(New England)

1 4-pound corned brisket of beef
1 bay leaf
(about 10) peppercorns
6 medium potatoes, peeled and cut into halves
6 carrots, scraped and cut into 2-inch lengths
2 large onions, peeled and cut into quarters
2 small turnips, pared and quartered
1 medium head of cabbage, cut into 6 wedges

Place corned brisket in Dutch oven and cover with water. Add bay leaf and peppercorns, and cook covered over moderate heat until boiling point is reached. Lower heat immediately and simmer for 2 hours. Then add potatoes, carrots, onions, turnips, and cabbage. Cover and allow to simmer for 45 minutes more or until meat and vegetables are tender. Arrange vegetables around the corned beef on a platter. Carve at the table and serve.

Serves 4 to 6

CHURCH SOCIAL STEW

(Midwest)

This dish is a mainstay of many a church Sunday supper night. The recipe has been cut down for home service.

2-1/2 pounds lean beef, cut into cubes
3 medium carrots, sliced
4 onions, peeled and quartered
1/2 pound fresh mushrooms, sliced
2 medium fresh tomatoes, cut into eighths
1 cup tomato juice
1 bay leaf
3 beef bouillon cubes
2 tablespoons brown sugar
1-1/2 teaspoons salt
freshly ground pepper
1-1/2 tablespoons quick-cooking Tapioca
4 cups cooked rice

Combine all ingredients in a 3-quart casserole and cover. Bake in a 275 degree oven for at least 4 hours, or until meat is fully tender. Serve over mounds of rice.

Serves 6 to 8

LAMB STEW

(Idaho)

This is a popular recipe on ranches where lambs are raised. The slow cooking brings out the bouquet of lamb combined with vegetables and seasonings.

2 tablespoons butter or margarine
2-1/2 pounds stewing lamb, cut into cubes with fat removed
1 teaspoon salt
freshly ground pepper
2 tablespoons flour
4 medium carrots, scraped and sliced
4 medium onions, quartered
4 potatoes, pared and cut in pieces
1/2 cauliflower (medium size) separated into flowerets
1/2 cup turnip, pared and diced

Melt butter or margarine in deep saucepan and add lamb. Brown cubes on all sides, and season with salt and pepper. Stir in flour and, when well blended, add water to cover. Cover and simmer for 1-1/4 hours, or until lamb is nearly tender. Add carrots, onions, potatoes, cauliflower, and turnip. Cover again and continue to simmer for 40 minutes longer.

Serves 6

HOPPIN' JOHN

(South Carolina)

A dish of blackeye peas is traditional on New Year's Day as a foretelling of good luck. Perhaps this dish is named as it is because it hopped right out of the original kitchens and became part of the repertoires of cooks all across the Southern states.

1/2 pound ham (1 piece)
3/4 cup dried and washed blackeye peas
3/4 cup (uncooked) rice
3/4 teaspoon salt

Place ham in 1 quart of cold water in a deep saucepan and cook over moderate heat. When water boils, begin to add blackeye peas; then cover pot, reduce heat, and simmer for 1-3/4 hours. Add rice and salt, cover again, and continue to simmer for about 35 minutes. When blackeye peas and rice are tender, remove ham and cut into chunks. Drain any remaining water from peas and rice. Mix ham through the peas and rice, and serve hot.

Serves 4 to 6

RED FLANNEL HASH

(Vermont)

You can take your pick of the stories (how many allegorical, which one true?) told of the origin of red flannel hash. I prefer to think that it was first formulated on a wintry night and that someone appreciatively remarked that it warmed the body as well as red flannel underwear.

4 tablespoons butter or margarine
1 pound ground chuck steak
3/4 teaspoon salt
freshly ground pepper
1 large potato, boiled and cut into small pieces
4 small cooked beets, finely chopped
1 medium onion, finely chopped
3 tablespoons heavy cream

Melt butter or margarine in a skillet over low heat and add ground meat, salt, and pepper. Stir in potato pieces, beets, and onion. Simmer over low heat for 10 minutes, stirring constantly. Add cream and stir through. Cover and simmer for 1/2 hour, stirring occasionally. Hash is done when a crust forms on the bottom. Fold in half like an omelet.

Serves 4

BASS STEW

(North Carolina)

A popular catch brought home by the Mr., put into a pot by the Mrs. and cooked as follows.

2 tablespoons butter or margarine
1 pound pork, defatted and diced
1 teaspoon salt
freshly ground pepper
2-1/2 pounds bass steaks, boned
3 medium onions, quartered
3 medium potatoes, pared and cut in pieces
3 tablespoons ketchup
dash of hot pepper sauce

In a Dutch oven, melt butter or margarine over low flame. Add pork and brown on all sides. Season with salt and pepper, and cover with water. Place lid on pot, simmer for 1-1/2 hours, and add bass. Cover and simmer for 1/2 hour longer. Then add onions and potatoes. Season with ketchup, stir well, and add hot pepper sauce. Simmer 45 minutes longer. Serve in soup plates with hot biscuits.

Serves 6

BEAN STEW

(Utah, Mormon)

For the Mormons, a filling souplike stew eaten with bread was often their complete meal. Following is one of the most popular stews.

1-1/4 cups red kidney beans
1-1/4 cups dried lima beans
1 large onion, minced
1 pound pork, diced
1 cup canned tomatoes (drain liquid)
2 medium potatoes, pared and cut up
1 teaspoon salt
freshly ground pepper
1/4 teaspoon hot pepper sauce
1/2 teaspoon thyme
2 tablespoons ketchup
1-1/2 pounds bacon, crisp and crumbled

Soak kidney and lima beans together in water to cover, allowing to remain overnight in a large, deep saucepan. Add onion, pork, canned tomatoes, and potatoes to beans and liquid, and season with salt, pepper, hot pepper sauce, thyme, and ketchup. Stir well and simmer for 2-1/2 hours, or until beans are tender. Stir in bacon crumbs and serve.

Serves 6

OXTAIL HANGOVER STEW

(Western)

Some who too freely imbibe alcoholic beverages claim that this recipe is restorative to those who have overindulged. Whether this is true, or the clear Rocky Mountain-swept air has more to do with their recovery, it's still a good dish.

2 tablespoons butter or margarine
3-1/2 pounds oxtails, cut into 2-inch pieces with fat trimmed off
1 teaspoon salt
freshly ground pepper
3 cans beer
1/8 teaspoon hot pepper sauce
1 teaspoon Worcestershire sauce
1 egg, lightly beaten
2 medium onions, quartered
3 medium potatoes, pared and cut into pieces
4 carrots, scraped and sliced

Melt butter in Dutch oven. Add oxtails and brown over low flame. Season with salt and pepper. Add beer, hot pepper sauce, and Worcestershire sauce. Stir egg into mixture until completely blended with other ingredients. Cover and continue simmering for 2-1/4 hours, or until oxtails are nearly tender. Add onions, potatoes, and carrots and simmer 40 minutes longer.

Serves 4 to 6

P.S.: You don't *have* to have a hangover to enjoy it!

JAMBALAYA

(New Orleans)

This is one of those recipes that became authentically American through the years. Toward the end of the eighteenth century, it was a Spanish recipe, but when Creole cooks added their special flavorings and technique, Jambalaya became an all-American original.

1/4 cup butter or margarine
1 pound cooked ham, diced
1/4 medium green pepper, finely chopped
1 medium onion, finely chopped
1-1/2 pounds cooked and cleaned shrimp
2 cups canned tomatoes, with liquid
1/2 can tomato paste (1/4 cup)
1 teaspoon salt
freshly ground pepper
1/4 teaspoon hot pepper sauce
1 clove garlic, minced
1 teaspoon thyme
1 tablespoon chopped parsley
1 bay leaf
1-1/2 cups cooked rice

In a skillet, melt butter or margarine over low heat and stir in ham, green pepper, and onion. Continue stirring and, after 7 minutes, add shrimp and canned tomatoes, liquid, and tomato paste. Season with salt, pepper, hot pepper sauce, garlic, thyme, and parsley. Place bay leaf in the liquid, and continue to heat and stir for about 5 minutes. Cover and simmer for 8 minutes more. Serve over mounds of fluffy rice.

Serves 4

Fish and Shellfish

CODFISH CAKES WITH POACHED EGGS

(Connecticut)

Many Connecticut cooks serve codfish cakes and poached eggs as a special Sunday breakfast treat. Salt cod was once practically New England coinage, when ship captains exchanged the fish for West Indies rum.

1 pound salt cod
5 medium potatoes (about 2 pounds)
milk for whipping potatoes
1/4 pound butter or margarine
freshly ground pepper
2 eggs
1-1/2 tablespoons coriander

1/4 teaspoon garlic powder
6 eggs
parsley sprigs

It is necessary to freshen the cod. Soak it in cold water for at least 6 hours, changing the water every hour, if possible. Drain and rinse the fish. Remove any pieces of bone and skin. Place the cod, with water to cover, in a saucepan. Simmer over low heat for about 25 minutes, or until fish flakes easily.

While fish is cooking, peel potatoes, cut into chunks, and parboil in a deep saucepan for about 25 minutes, or until soft. Turn off heat and add milk, one-half the butter, and pepper. Mash and whip the potatoes to a soft consistency, adding milk a little at a time, as needed.

In a mixing bowl, combine fish and potatoes and break in eggs, mixing well. Season with coriander and garlic. Blend well and shape into flat round cakes about 2/3 inch thick.

Melt remaining butter in a skillet over low heat and place fish cakes in pan. Brown on each side—about 4-1/2 minutes on the first side and about 3 minutes more on the other.

Serve with a poached egg atop each cake. Eggs should be prepared for poaching by breaking each into a saucer, and then sliding the egg into a large saucepan in which slightly vinegared water is briskly boiling. Immediately turn off the heat and allow to stand for 5 minutes. Remove eggs with a slotted spoon and place one egg on each codfish cake. Garnish with a sprig of parsley.

Serves 6

CODFISH BALLS

(Massachusetts)

1 pound codfish, boned, skinned, and cut into pieces
1 teaspoon salt
3-1/2 cups cooked mashed potatoes
1/2 teaspoon dill
1 tablespoon onion powder
2 eggs
1 cup bread crumbs
oil for frying

Place codfish in cold water in a saucepan over moderate heat. Bring to boiling point. Cover and reduce heat. Simmer about 12 minutes, or until fish flakes easily. Remove fish and flake into a large mixing bowl. Add warm mashed potatoes and season with dill and onion powder, mixing well. Beat in eggs. Form balls between moist fingers (about 1-inch in diameter) and roll balls in bread crumbs. Heat oil in a skillet over low heat. When oil temperature reaches 350 degrees, drop balls from spoon into skillet, turning each once. When brown, after about 1 minute, remove balls to paper towel to drain. A portion is usually 4 balls.

Serves 4 to 6

FOURTH OF JULY TRADITIONAL SALMON AND EGG SAUCE

(New England)

From the moment word of adoption of the Declaration of Independence spread throughout the Colonies, special celebrations were organized throughout New England. What better culinary accompaniment to the festivities than the eastern salmon beginning their "run," and what more appropriate food to signify the newness of independence than the young green peas and the first of the potato crop?

1 4 to 5 pound piece of fresh salmon (cut from center of the fish)
cheesecloth
1 bay leaf
4 peppercorns
2 lemons, cut into wedges
1 teaspoon salt

Wash salmon and wrap in a piece of cheesecloth, securing the open ends with tied strings. Do not cut ends of string, but leave long to facilitate removal of the fish after it is cooked. Place wrapped salmon in a deep saucepan, with water to cover, over moderate heat. Add bay leaf, peppercorns, lemon wedges, and salt.

When water shows signs of beginning to boil, lower heat at once, cover, and simmer for 45 minutes. Fish flakes easily when fully cooked. Remove at once from heat. Place on serving platter, and skin and bone, if desired.

While salmon cooks, prepare the:

EGG SAUCE

1-1/2 cups milk
1/2 cup heavy cream
1 small onion, thinly sliced
1/2 teaspoon salt
freshly ground pepper
4 tablespoons butter or margarine
4 tablespoons flour
3 hard-boiled eggs, coarsely chopped
capers
parsley sprigs

In a saucepan, over moderate flame, heat milk and cream with onion slices, salt, pepper, and butter. Stir constantly and, when butter has melted, add the flour slowly, so that sauce will be smooth. Then add chopped eggs and mix well. Turn sauce into a gravy boat or a bowl, and sprinkle capers across the surface. Place parsley about the salmon. Serve the fish with sauce accompanying it and, if you are a true traditionalist, serve new potatoes and tender green peas.

Serves 4 to 6

CATFISH FRY

(Texas)

1 pound catfish fillets
1 teaspoon salt
freshly ground pepper
1 teaspoon paprika
2 eggs
2 tablespoons water
1 cup cornmeal
3 tablespoons butter

Sprinkle fillets with salt, pepper, and paprika. Beat eggs and stir in water. Spread cornmeal on a board. Roll each piece of fish in the cornmeal. Next dip it into the egg, then roll again in cornmeal. Refrigerate fish for about 20 minutes. Melt butter in a skillet over low heat and fry fish for about 3 minutes on first side; turn and fry for 2 minutes more, adding more butter if needed. Serve with hush puppies.

Serves 4

BROILED SALMON

(Alaska)

This fish contains much fat, and it was salmon fat, as well as the blubber of seals, that sustained the Eskimos living farthest north.

1/2 teaspoon salt
freshly ground pepper
juice of 1 lemon
4 salmon steaks
1-1/2 tablespoons melted butter or margarine

Sprinkle salt, pepper, and lemon juice over salmon steaks and brush them with melted butter or margarine. Place in a lightly greased pan under the broiler and allow 5 minutes on top side; turn and broil 4 more minutes.

Serves 4

BAKED POTOMAC SPRING SHAD

(District of Columbia)

George Washington recognized and enjoyed good food. To supply his kitchen with fish, he maintained several fishing posts along the Potomac and caught shad, one of his favorite fish. The shad might then be prepared for service to statesmen of the Republic on leisurely weekend sails down the Potomac.

1 3-pound roe shad, split and boned
1 teaspoon salt
freshly ground pepper
3 tablespoons butter or margarine
1 extra roe
1 teaspoon salt (for cooking roe)
1 tablespoon vinegar

Preheat oven to 400 degrees. Place fish, skin down, in greased baking pan. Season with salt and pepper. Dot with butter or margarine and bake for 35 minutes.

While shad is baking, prepare roe by placing in a deep saucepan, with water to cover, over moderate heat. Add salt and vinegar. Parboil by simmering for 12 minutes. Drain and cover roe with cold water. Allow to stand 5 minutes, then drain again. Remove membrane and separate eggs with fork. Set aside for sauce.

SAUCE

3 tablespoons butter or margarine
2 tablespoons flour
3/4 cup light cream
cooked roe
1/2 teaspoon salt
juice of 1 lemon
2 eggs, beaten
1/2 cup white wine

Melt butter or margarine in a saucepan over low heat and stir in flour, mixing well. Gradually stir in cream and roe while keeping heat low and stirring constantly. Season with salt and lemon juice. Then add eggs, stirring as you work, and stir in white wine.

Remove fish from oven and pour sauce over all.

Serves 6

BARBECUED COLUMBIA RIVER SALMON

(Oregon)

The fatted salmon swims from salty seawater into the freshwater river and battles its way upstream against the current; it is in the river that the salmon is caught.

6 large salmon steaks
1/4 cup olive oil
juice of 2 lemons
1 teaspoon onion powder
1/2 teaspoon salt
freshly ground pepper

Allow flame in grill to reach high heat. While fire is building, brush olive oil over fillets and sprinkle with lemon juice. Dust onion powder over all fish and season with salt and pepper. Spread aluminum foil across grill and place salmon steaks on this. Cover with a second sheet of foil. Cook 25 to 35 minutes, depending on the thickness of salmon. Fish is done when it can be flaked easily with a fork.

Serves 6

FISHERMAN'S HALIBUT BAKE

(Alaska)

4 halibut fillets, 1-inch thick
1 teaspoon salt
freshly ground pepper
2 tablespoons onion, chopped
1/2 green pepper, cut into strips
1/4 cup melted butter

Preheat oven to 400 degrees. Place fillets in a lightly greased baking dish. Season with salt and pepper, and sprinkle chopped onion and green pepper over fish. Brush melted butter on the fish and bake in 400 degree oven for 20 minutes, or until fish flakes easily with a fork.

Serves 4

CRAB LOUIS

(Seattle)

This is a manly salad, created by a local chef and originally given fame by the admiration of Enrico Caruso, who consumed a prodigious quantity of it. It remains a Pacific Northwest favorite and is known locally by the more familiar name Louie.

4 cups crab meat
1 teaspoon onion powder
3 tablespoons chili sauce
dash of cayenne
lettuce leaves
2 hard-boiled eggs, sliced
2 large tomatoes, sliced
1 medium cucumber, sliced
1 cup mayonnaise
paprika

In a mixing bowl, combine crab meat with onion powder, chili sauce, and cayenne. Mix well. Place lettuce leaves on individual plates and heap crab meat on the lettuce. Arrange sliced eggs, tomatoes, and cucumber around the crab meat. Spoon mayonnaise over the crab meat, and sprinkle paprika over the mayonnaise. Refrigerate until ready for use.

Serves 4

CLAMS AND RICE

(San Francisco)

This recipe is from that area where the foggy mists blow in from the Pacific Ocean, through the San Francisco Bay to Fisherman's Wharf.

2 tablespoons olive oil
3/4 cup scallions with green stems, sliced
1 small green pepper, diced
1/4 cup mushrooms, sliced
1/2 teaspoon garlic powder
1/4 teaspoon fennel
1/4 teaspoon salt
freshly ground pepper
1 cup uncooked rice
2 cups canned tomatoes and liquid
1 cup tomato juice
2 quarts clams, opened and washed
parsley sprigs
lemon wedges

Pour olive oil into a Dutch oven and, over low heat, sauté scallions, green pepper, and mushrooms. Season with garlic, fennel, salt, and pepper. Add rice, canned tomatoes (including liquid), and tomato juice. Add clams and sufficient water to cover. Keep heat low and simmer for 30 minutes, or until rice and clams are tender. (Cut a bit off a clam to judge.) Serve in soup plates and garnish with parsley. Serve with lemon wedges.

Serves 4 to 6

FRISCO OYSTER TUNNEL

(San Francisco)

1 loaf fresh french bread
3/4 cup melted butter

Preheat oven to 400 degrees. Using a long knife, scoop out dough in the center of length of bread, after cutting off one end to gain access. Brush the interior of loaf with melted butter. Toast bread in over for 12 minutes.

2 tablespoons butter or margarine
2 dozen medium oysters, without shells
4 eggs
1 cup dry bread crumbs
1 small chili pepper, minced
1 cup sliced mushrooms
2 tablespoons tomato sauce

Melt butter or margarine in a skillet over low flame and quickly cook oysters, allowing no more than 1 minute each side. Break eggs into pan; add bread crumbs, chili pepper, mushrooms, and tomato sauce. Remove from heat as soon as eggs are firm, and fill bread cavity. Place in oven 5 minutes (400 degrees)—no longer!

To serve, cut into slices and serve with chili sauce, Worcestershire sauce, or ketchup.

Serves 4

OYSTERS ROCKEFELLER

(New Orleans)

According to legend, this recipe was named by an 1899 diner at Antoine's famous New Orleans restaurant who declared it to be "as rich as Rockefeller."

4 tablespoons butter or margarine
4 tablespoons raw spinach, finely chopped
1 medium stalk of celery, thinly sliced
1/4 small onion, minced
dash of hot pepper sauce
1/4 teaspoon salt
3-1/2 tablespoons dry, fine bread crumbs
24 oysters on the half shell
parsley sprigs

Melt butter or margarine in a saucepan over low heat. Add spinach, celery, and onion and season with hot pepper sauce and salt. Add bread crumbs and stir thoroughly. Allow to simmer, while stirring, for 10 minutes. Remove from heat and chop to a paste, or force through a coarse strainer. Place a scant teaspoonful atop each oyster with a dab of butter on paste. Broil for 3 to 4 minutes, and serve at once. Garnish with parsley sprigs.

Serves 4

HANGTOWN FRY

(California)

Take your pick of what to believe about the beginnings of this recipe; there are several legends. One says that this was the last requested meal of a condemned prisoner, selected by him because both oysters and eggs were hard to come by. The second version has a gold rich miner demanding the most expensive dish in town and plunking down $1,500 in gold nuggets to pay for it.

5 eggs
3/4 cup fine, dry bread crumbs
2 dozen small oysters, without shells
2-1/2 tablespoons butter or margarine
1 teaspoon salt
freshly ground pepper

Break one of the eggs into a bowl and beat lightly. Set aside and spread bread crumbs across a board. Roll oysters in crumbs and dip each oyster into beaten egg, then again in the crumbs.

Melt butter in skillet over low flame. Add oysters and cook no more than a minute on each side. Break the remaining eggs into the egg bowl (any crumbs won't hurt) and beat lightly. Add salt and pepper. Pour eggs over oysters. Cook like an omelet, allowing runny egg to reach heated pan by lifting the congealed egg with a spatula. Turn to brown upper side. Serve with fried sausages or bacon, if desired.

Serves 4

DOWN-EAST BROILED SOFT-SHELL CRABS

(New England)

Be certain that your fish dealer has fully cleaned the crabs or clean them yourself. To clean, kill them with the sharp point of a small knife inserted into the body between the eyes. Raise and cut off the tapered points of the back shell and clean away the spongy material beneath. Place the crab on its back and cut off the part at the back of the shell called the apron, and cut off the face.

8 soft-shell crabs
1/2 teaspoon salt
freshly ground pepper
juice of 1 lemon
3 tablespoons butter

Place the crabs in a greased metal pan and season each side with salt, pepper, and lemon juice. Dot with butter and broil until browned (about 4 minutes on each side).

Serves 4

LOBSTER AND CHICKEN CREOLE

(New Orleans)

4 tablespoons butter or margarine
1 3-pound chicken, cut into serving pieces
1 clove garlic, minced
2 medium onions, coarsely chopped
1 green pepper, chopped
2 cups celery, chopped
1/4 teaspoon hot pepper sauce
1/2 teaspoon salt
freshly ground pepper
1 teaspoon thyme
1 bay leaf
2 cups canned tomatoes
1 6-ounce can tomato paste
3/4 pound cooked lobster meat, cut into small pieces
2-1/2 cups cooked rice

Melt butter or margarine in a skillet over low flame and sauté chicken pieces until all sides are browned. Remove chicken and set aside. Place garlic, onions, green pepper, and celery in skillet and sauté. season with hot pepper sauce, salt, pepper, thyme, and bay leaf. Stir well, and add tomatoes and tomato paste. Return chicken to skillet and cover. Cook slowly for 40 minutes, turning chicken pieces once during cooking. Add lobster meat, cover, and simmer for 7 minutes more. Caution: Do not overcook lobster.

Serve in soup plates over a mound of rice.

Serves 6

RED SNAPPER BAKE

(Northwest)

4 slices red snapper, boned and skinned
1 medium onion, chopped
1 teaspoon salt
freshly ground pepper
2 tablespoons flour
1 cup sour cream
1/2 cup shredded Monterey Jack cheese

Preheat oven to 350 degrees. Grease a baking dish and place the slices of fish across it, laying them flat. Spread onion over the fish, and season with salt and pepper. Sprinkle flour across the fish and pour sour cream over all. Bake for 25 minutes. Sprinkle cheese over fish and bake for an additional 10 minutes.

Serves 4

STEAMED CLAMS

(Connecticut)

There are littleneck, quahog, cherrystone, soft shell, steamer, and many lesser known varieties of clam. Each is a delicacy. Be sure to wash them under cold running water, to remove all bits of sand. *Never* use clams that smell bad, and you can always be sure of fresh clams.

1 quart clams
1 teaspoon garlic powder
freshly ground pepper
1/4 teaspoon dill
1 teaspoon basil
1/2 cup sherry
1/4 pound butter or margarine
juice of 1-1/2 lemons
1 tablespoon chopped parsley

Place clams in a deep saucepan and season with garlic powder, pepper, dill, basil, and sherry. Cover and place over high heat for about 7 minutes, when pot will be filled with steam. Lower heat and steam for 10 minutes, after which shells will open. Note: Do not lift cover of pot during steaming process.

Extract clams from shells and, in a small saucepan, melt butter over low heat and stir in lemon juice.

Serve clams in soup plates with some of the broth (which may be strained). Accompany with melted butter. Garnish with chopped parsley.

Serves 4

NANTUCKET SCALLOPS

(Massachusetts)

2 pounds bay scallops (the small ones)
1 teaspoon paprika
1 teaspoon salt
1/4 teaspoon white pepper
1 cup soda cracker crumbs
1/4 teaspoon garlic powder
2 tablespoons butter or margarine, melted

Combine all other ingredients except butter or margarine in a mixing bowl and roll scallops in the mixture. Place coated scallops in a lightly greased broiling pan and pour melted butter over all. Broil for no more than 7 minutes.

Serves 4 to 6

SOLE, SAUSAGE, AND EGGS

(California)

1/2 pound sausage, sliced
4 small pieces fillet of sole
1/2 teaspoon salt
freshly ground pepper
4 eggs
parsley sprigs

In a skillet over moderate heat, cook sausage until browned. No additional fat is needed in the skillet. Add fillets of sole. Season fish with salt and pepper, and cook 4 minutes on each side. Place on heated platter with sausage. Break eggs into pan and cook. Arrange on 4 plates; place sausage on top of each piece of fish and one egg atop the sausage. Garnish with parsley sprigs.

Serves 4

FILBERT FISH FILLET

(Oregon)

Filberts are one of the large crops in Oregon and are included in many recipes.

4 tablespoons butter or margarine
4 pieces fillet of sole
1/4 cup chopped celery
1/4 cup filberts, chopped
1/4 teaspoon salt
freshly ground pepper
2 tablespoons heavy cream

In a skillet over low heat melt butter or margarine and add fillets, celery, and filberts. Season with salt and pepper. Cook for 4 minutes, turn fish, and cook for 4 more minutes. Remove fish to heated plates and mix cream into pan liquid with the chopped filberts. Spoon sauce over fish.

Serves 4

CAPE COD TURKEY
(not turkey at all, but codfish)

(Massachusetts)

1-1/2 pounds salt codfish
freshly ground pepper
1/2 pound salt pork, sliced
6 medium potatoes, peeled and boiled

Cover salt codfish with water and soak for about 6 hours. If possible, change water hourly.

Place fish in a deep saucepan with fresh water to cover. Simmer over low heat for 25 minutes. Drain. Remove skin and any bones. Sprinkle pepper on fish.

In a greased skillet, over moderate heat, cook salt pork slices until browned and crisp. Drain.

Place some codfish, salt pork, and a boiled potato on each plate. Spoon over a scant amount of the salt pork fat to moisten.

Serves 6

BROILED LOBSTER

(Maine)

4 prepared lobsters, 1-1/2 to 2 pounds each
(Have your fish dealer make the kill and clean the lobsters.)
1/2 pound butter, melted
lemon wedges

Preheat broiler for about 10 minutes. Place lobsters, shell down on grill. Brush meat with a little of the melted butter. Broil for 10 minutes, basting occasionally. Place remaining melted butter in a small bowl for dipping, and serve lemon wedges with each portion. Serve lobsters immediately, providing each diner with a bib or huge napkin to tuck under the chin. Serve with a nutcracker accompanying each lobster and an oyster fork for manipulating the flesh in the claws.

Serves 4

Birds and Fowl

BENJAMIN FRANKLIN regretted that the turkey hadn't been established as our national bird, rather than the bald eagle. In a way, the turkey is quasi-officially the American bird. It is served on most every family's table on Thanksgiving, and on other holidays as well.

When the pilgrims arrived on the shores of the land they would eventually call New England, they found wild turkeys in abundance, and the abundance of the birds helped them to survive. The forests were full of turkey cocks' calls from the first faint light of dawn until sunup. The wood cushioned many other calls, such as those of the more muted passenger pigeons, which were once probably more abundant than any other bird or animal on this continent and were considered delicious. Perhaps they were too flavorsome for their own good, for they are now extinct.

Unfortunately, the newly arrived settlers not

only made inroads upon the land, but also decimated huge flocks of birds, as well as edible raccoons, bears, gray squirrels, and opossums.

Toward the end of the eighteenth century, the plight of Connecticut's Mohegan Indians had grown desperate—the tribe found their natural larders of river, land, and sea gone bare. Nor was there any longer the lavish growth of nuts, beans, and fruits to sustain them. The Mohegans were reduced to make appeal to the spoilers for sufficient food to survive.

We must beware lest this be a lesson unlearned. Each Thanksgiving, as we partake of our traditional roast turkey, we might set aside time for reflection on nature's bounties and on man's diminution of all nature's wealth.

NEW ENGLAND ROAST TURKEY

(Vermont)

1 8 to 10 pound turkey (1 pound per person will be more than sufficient to allow for leftovers)
1 teaspoon salt
freshly ground pepper
1 tablespoon butter or margarine (optional)

STUFFING

30 slices day-old bread
1-1/4 teaspoons salt
1 teaspoon sage
1/8 teaspoon nutmeg
2 eggs, well beaten
1-3/4 cups warm water
3-inch cube of fat salt pork, chopped
1/4-pound sausage, chopped

Have your butcher clean the turkey thoroughly, removing lungs and other organs, as well as the oil sac above the tail. Remove any remaining pin feathers and, if any hairs remain on wings or legs, singe them over your stove burner. Make sure the organs have all been cut from the cavity and remove any excessive wads of fat. Wash the bird inside and out before preparing to roast.

If desired, simmer neck, heart, liver, and gizzard in water to cover and use these, minced, in stuffing or gravy.

In a mixing bowl, crumble the slices of bread into coarse crumbs. Add seasonings of salt, sage, and nutmeg and gradually stir in warm water and pieces of salt pork and sausage. Stir in beaten eggs. Mix all ingredients thoroughly.

Preheat oven to 325 degrees. Stuff turkey just before you are ready to roast it. Put large spoonfuls of stuffing into body cavity. Do not pack tightly, as stuffing expands during roasting. Stuff neck opening to give turkey a fully rounded breast. Sew openings together, or use skewers and lace with strings.

Apply butter to the skin only if the turkey lacks fat. Sprinkle on salt and pepper. Place breast side up on a rack in a roasting pan and roast. Place aluminum foil in a tent-like shape over bird. If your oven is electric, do not allow foil to come in contact with the heating element. Allow 4 to 4-1/2 hours roasting time and baste as it roasts. About 3/4 of an hour before roasting is done, remove foil and allow the turkey to brown. It is done when the leg can be easily moved up and down. Allow turkey to remain on a heat-resistant platter in opened oven for the next 1/2 hour to ensure greater ease in carving.

GRAVY

1-1/2 cups boiling water
1/2 cup pan drippings
3 tablespoons flour
3/4 cup boiling water

Add boiling water to pan drippings. Place pan over low heat across two burners on stove top. Stir and scrape the encrusted drippings. Gradually add flour and continue to stir while you add 3/4 cup more water. Cook for 3 more minutes and serve in a gravy boat or bowl with a ladle for individual service. The turkey should be carved at the table and the stuffing then removed from the bird.

Note: Do not refrigerate leftover turkey with any of the stuffing still in the bird.

Serves 8

MR. JEFFERSON'S SQUAB

(Virginia)

1-1/2 tablespoons butter or margarine
4 squabs, cleaned (Cornish hens may be substituted)
1 large onion, minced
1 cup celery, chopped
1 teaspoon salt
1/2 cup fresh sliced mushrooms
1/2 cup sherry

Melt butter in a large Dutch oven over moderate heat. Add squabs, then, immediately, the onion and celery. Salt the ingredients. Cover pot and turn birds every 10 minutes until skin is entirely browned to just a glow (that is, not crisp). After 40 minutes, add mushrooms and pour sherry over the birds. Cover and cook for 10 minutes. Serve an entire bird to each guest. Turnips and a green salad make a good accompaniment.

Serves 4

PACIFIC ROAST TURKEY

(Oregon)

Throughout the Northwest, large turkey flocks are herded on ranches. At about nine months of age, they are brought to market.

For the purpose of ingredient proportions in the stuffing, it will be assumed that you are roasting an 8 to 10 pound turkey. Follow all instructions for preparation and roasting as given in recipe for New England Roast Turkey. It is the stuffing that creates the regional difference.

PACIFIC OYSTER STUFFING

1-1/2 pints large Pacific oysters, cut into pieces
juice of 1 lemon
6 cups bread crumbs
1/2 cup chopped celery
1 small onion, minced
1 teaspoon salt
1-1/2 cups water
1 egg, beaten

In a mixing bowl, blend all other ingredients and slowly add water and the egg. Mix and stuff the turkey.

Prepare gravy as for New England Roast Turkey.

CHICKEN FRICASSEE

(Mississippi)

1 3 pound chicken, cut into serving pieces
1 teaspoon salt
freshly ground pepper
1 egg, well beaten
1/2 cup soda crackers, crumbled
oil for frying
1 cup hot water
2 cups cooked rice
3 fresh tomatoes, chopped
1 small green pepper, minced

Season chicken with salt and pepper. Break egg and beat in a small wide bowl. Spread cracker crumbs on a board. Dip each piece of chicken in egg and dip in crumbs. Place oil in skillet and heat. Fry chicken pieces until golden brown. When sufficiently browned on all sides, add hot water and place cover on skillet. Simmer over low heat for 45 minutes, or until chicken is tender. Remove chicken pieces to a platter and add cooked rice to skillet juices, then tomatoes, and green pepper. Cover and cook for 10 minutes. Bring to the table on a large serving platter with chicken heaped in center and bordered by rice.

Serves 4 or 5

FRIED CHICKEN

(Maryland)

2 eggs
3 tablespoons water
1-2/3 cups fine cracker crumbs
1 teaspoon salt
freshly ground pepper
1 3-pound chicken, cut into serving pieces
cooking oil

In a bowl, beat eggs until lemony and add water, mixing well. Spread cracker crumbs on a board, and sprinkle salt and pepper over the crumbs. Lightly moisten chicken pieces and roll in the cracker crumbs. Then dip each piece in the eggs and again roll all sides in the crumbs. Repeat procedure for each piece of chicken. Place on a platter and refrigerate for 15 minutes to set the crumbs.

In a skillet over moderate heat, pour cooking oil to a depth of 1-1/2 inches. Place fleshier pieces of chicken in oil first, skin side down. Use tongs or two spoons as a vise to turn pieces in oil. When all pieces are browned, add 2 or 3 tablespoons water. Lower heat and cover. Cook for 30 minutes, then remove cover. Allow 15 to 20 minutes of further cooking. Drain on paper toweling and serve hot.

Serves 6

STIFLED CHICKEN AND OYSTERS

(Martha's Vineyard)

In New England the land and sea were married over 200 years ago in the combination of chicken and oysters.

4 tablespoons butter or margarine
1 3-1/2 pound chicken, cut into serving pieces
1 teaspoon salt
freshly ground pepper
1-1/2 tablespoons flour
1-1/4 cups milk
1 quart fresh oysters, drained
1 cup light cream

In a skillet, melt butter or margarine over low heat and place chicken pieces in pan. Season with salt and pepper. Brown on all sides. Remove and place the chicken in a greased casserole. Preheat oven to 325 degrees. Mix flour in pan juices and, stirring well, cook until liquid thickens. Slowly stir in the milk and pour mixture over the chicken. Cover and bake for 1 hour, then add oysters and pour cream over all. Bake 15 minutes longer, uncovered. Serve at once.

Serves 6

COUNTRY CAPTAIN

(Savannah, Georgia)

Whether a ship's captain took up residence in the Georgian countryside, or the story of this recipe being adapted from an East Indian dish is allegorical, the recipe has been faithfully handed down through the generations.

1/4 cup sifted all-purpose flour
1-1/2 teaspoons salt
freshly ground pepper
1 2-1/2 pound chicken, cut into serving pieces
1/4 cup butter or margarine
1 medium onion, chopped
1 medium green pepper, chopped
1 clove garlic, crushed
1 tablespoon curry powder
1 can (1 pound) tomatoes, with liquid
1/2 cup currants
1/4 cup blanched, roasted almonds
4 cups cooked rice
chutney

In a small bowl, combine flour, salt, and pepper and coat chicken pieces. Melt butter in skillet over low heat. Brown chicken, turning pieces occasionally. Remove chicken when browned, and sauté onion and green pepper, adding crushed garlic and curry powder. Return chicken to skillet and add tomatoes (broken into pieces) with liquid. Cover and cook for 35 minutes, or until chicken is tender. At last moment, add currants and almonds, stirring these through the liquid. Serve over hot rice with chutney.

Serves 4 to 6

FRIED CHICKEN

(Tennessee)

1 egg, beaten
1/4 cup milk
1 3-pound chicken, cut into serving pieces
3/4 cup all-purpose flour
1 teaspoon salt
freshly ground pepper
1/2 teaspoon tarragon
1 teaspoon paprika
oil for frying

In a wide-rimmed bowl, beat egg into milk. Dip chicken pieces into this mixture. Spread flour, salt, pepper, and tarragon across a board and dip all sides of chicken pieces in it. Rub paprika over each chicken piece. Heat oil in a skillet over low heat. Add chicken and fry, turning each piece occasionally, until all sides are browned and crisp, about 35 minutes. Allow chicken pieces to drain on paper toweling and serve.

Serves 4 to 6

WINE HERB-BAKED CHICKEN

(Western)

4 chicken breasts, split and boned
1/4 cup dry vermouth
1/4 cup lemon juice
2 tablespoons chopped parsley
1 teaspoon garlic powder
1 teaspoon salt
freshly ground pepper
1 teaspoon sage
1/2 teaspoon tarragon
1/2 teaspoon grated lemon peel
1 tablespoon paprika
1/2 cup warm water
1/4 cup all-purpose flour

In a large mixing bowl, place chicken breasts in mixture of vermouth, lemon juice, parsley, garlic powder, salt, pepper, sage, tarragon, lemon peel, and paprika. In a separate bowl, combine water and flour until paste is smooth. Add this to larger bowl and mix well. Place chicken in bowl and cover with plastic wrap, sealing all edges tightly. Turn chicken pieces at least once, to coat all sides. Allow chicken to marinate overnight in the refrigerator. Preheat oven to 375 degrees. Lightly grease baking dish and place chicken pieces in it. Pour over marinade. Bake for 45 minutes, or until chicken is fork-tender.

Serves 4

RITZY HEN

(New York City)

There was once a great New York hotel called the Ritz-Carlton, long since demolished, renowned for its culinary achievements. Here's one for a chicken putting on the ritz. Actually, it can be made with leftover chicken.

3 cups chicken, cooked and diced
1/4 cup mayonnaise
1/2 cup heavy cream
1 teaspoon salt
1 medium onion, minced
2 egg yolks, crumbled (hard cooked)
3-1/2 tablespoons grated Parmesan cheese

Place chicken in the top of a double boiler over boiling water and quickly mix in mayonnaise and cream, stirring quickly with a light hand. Add salt and onion. Cover and allow to heat thoroughly. Serve on toast points with rice, or with no accompaniment other than a green vegetable (fresh asparagus would be ideal). Remove from pot. Sprinkle egg crumbs over each portion and dust with Parmesan cheese.

Serves 3 to 4

CHICKEN AND DUMPLINGS

(Maine)

1 3-1/2 pound chicken, cut into serving pieces (reserve liver)
1 medium onion, chopped
2 stalks celery (with leaves), chopped
1 bay leaf
1 tablespoon parsley flakes
1-1/2 teaspoon salt
freshly ground pepper
dumplings (recipe follows)

Place chicken, with water to cover, in a Dutch oven. Add remaining ingredients and cover pot, cooking over moderate heat until boiling point is reached. At this time, skim foam from water, recover pot, lower heat, and simmer for 2-1/4 hours, when chicken should be tender. Cut liver into small pieces. Add liver and dumplings to pot. Cover and simmer for 15 minutes more. Increase heat to moderate until liquid boils, lower heat, and continue to simmer for 5 minutes.

DUMPLINGS

1 3/4 cups all-purpose flour
2 teaspoons baking powder
1 teaspoon salt
1 tablespoon shortening
1/2 cup milk

Sift flour into a mixing bowl with baking powder and salt. Add shortening and cut with pastry blender or two dull knives until dough resembles hard kernels. Stir lightly as you add milk. Dough should then be of a firm enough consistency to drop scant tablespoonfuls into chicken liquid.

Serves 6

ROAST DUCK WITH ORANGE SAUCE

(Virginia)

Although most ducks for home roasting are now purchased in the poultry section of butcher shops, and hunting of ducks has become a sportsman's hobby, in the early days of this country (and indeed, before we became a nation), duck hunting was one way of food gathering. The early settlers learned from the Indians the method of using decoys to attract the migrating birds. These were originally fashioned of bound bulrushes decorated with paint and feathers to approximate the shape and colored feathering of the wild ducks.

Recipes for roast duck have been carried down through the years.

1 5-6 pound duck, cleaned
3/4 teaspoon salt
freshly ground pepper
4 tablespoons butter or margarine
1 cup warm water
2 large apples, chopped with skin (cored)
3 teaspoons sugar
1/4 cup celery, thinly sliced
1/2 teaspoon salt
1 teaspoon onion powder

In a deep saucepan, melt butter or margarine in warm water. Stir in apples, sugar, and celery and season with salt and onion powder. After no more than 5 minutes of cooking, remove, toss lightly, and drain excess water. Rub cavity of duck with salt and pepper. Place stuffing loosely in duck. (If stuffing is left over, it may be dotted with butter and baked while the duck roasts, in a greased, covered baking dish.) Preheat oven to 400 degrees. Make small incisions for fat to run off in the skin of lower breast, back, and thighs. During roasting do not baste duck, and ladle off the fat accumulated in the pan several times. Place breast up on rock in roasting pan, and roast for 1/2 hour, then reduce heat to 325 degrees and roast 3/4 of an hour to 1 hour longer. When duck is done, it will be nicely browned and legs will be pliant and move easily.

ORANGE SAUCE

1/2 cup orange juice
1/2 cup beef bouillon or chicken stock
2 teaspoons orange rind
2 tablespoons sherry

Blend all ingredients in a saucepan over low heat. Remove as soon as liquid is heated. Do not allow to come to a boil.

Remove stuffing from duck, and serve duck quartered. Spoon sauce over individual servings.

Serves 4

STEWED CHICKEN

(Southern)

Nowhere is chicken better handled than in the Southern states. This is because many of the recipes were formulated by black slaves on the plantations, and these superb cooks were adapting their own most favored African recipes. In Africa it was an honor for a guest to be served a chicken dish.

1 3-1/2 pound chicken, cut into serving pieces
oil for frying
1 teaspoon salt
freshly ground pepper
2 medium onions, coarsely chopped
3 medium tomatoes, washed and chopped
3 cups hot water
1-1/2 tablespoons flour
dash of hot pepper sauce
1 teaspoon thyme
1/2 teaspoon tarragon
1/2 teaspoon garlic powder

Place chicken pieces in heated oil in a skillet and brown on all sides. Add salt, pepper, onions, tomatoes, and water. Cover and cook over low heat for 40 minutes. In a smaller skillet, pour off about 1/2 cup of the cooking liquid and stir in flour, blending well. Add hot pepper sauce, thyme, tarragon, and garlic powder. Return this mixture to the larger skillet. Simmer, uncovered, for 20 additional minutes.

Serves 6

CHICKEN LOAF

(Midwest)

1 3-pound chicken, cooked
2 cups bread crumbs
3 eggs, well beaten
3/4 cup chicken broth
1/2 cup catsup
1 tablespoon prepared mustard
1 teaspoon celery seed
1 teaspoon onion powder
1/8 teaspoon garlic powder
1/2 teaspoon mace
1 tablespoon chopped parsley

Cook chicken by whatever method you prefer (leftover chicken is ideal). Discard skin and chop or grind boned chicken. Place ground chicken in a mixing bowl, and add all other ingredients, and blend well. Preheat oven to 350 degrees. Lightly grease baking pan and mold chicken mixture into a loaf shape. Lightly indent the skin of the long loaf and sprinkle chopped parsley over this indentation. Bake for 55 minutes, or until loaf is somewhat crusty.

Serves 6

MONROE CHICKEN PUDDING

(Eastern)

Monroe's doctrine is internationally famous. President James Monroe's family was nourished by recipes such as this.

1 3-pound chicken, cut into serving pieces
1 teaspoon salt
freshly ground pepper
1 teaspoon sage

BATTER

1-1/2 cups all-purpose flour
1/4 teaspoon salt
4 eggs
1-1/2 cups milk

Season chicken with salt, pepper, and sage. Add chicken to greased skillet over low heat, cover, and cook for 25 minutes, or until chicken is tender. Remove chicken to a greased baking dish. Preheat oven to 425 degrees. Prepare batter in a mixing bowl by sifting flour with salt. Beat in eggs and gradually add milk, beating hard. When batter is of a firm, elastic consistency, pour it over chicken pieces and bake for 20 minutes. Lower heat to 375 degrees and continue baking for 20 minutes more. At this time, batter should be puffed and brown. Serve hot with a salad and green vegetables.

Serves 4 to 6

POTTED PHEASANT

(New Jersey)

The pheasant is native to China, and it was the English seafarers who introduced it to America, where Benjamin Franklin's son-in-law enthusiastically raised the birds on his New Jersey farmland.

1 3-pound pheasant, cleaned
2 teaspoons salt
4 strips bacon, uncooked
2-1/2 tablespoons butter or margarine
2 apples, pared, cored, and sliced
1 pint berries (your selection)
1 cup sliced fresh mushrooms
1 cup red wine

Rub bird with half the salt into the cavity and the remaining salt into skin. Place strips of bacon across bird. Melt butter or margarine in a Dutch oven over low heat. Place pheasant in pot and surround it with apples, berries, and mushrooms. Pour wine over all. Cover pot and simmer over low heat for 1-1/2 hours. Check every 15 minutes to make certain there is sufficient moisture in the pot and, at the same time, baste bird with pot juices. Add more wine or water if needed. If it is desired to crisp skin, preheat oven to 375 degrees and place bird, surrounded by the fruits, mushrooms, and drippings, in a lightly greased pan. Roast for about 10 to 12 minutes. Serve with a side dish of rice, assorted vegetables, and a salad.

Serves 4

ROAST GUINEA HEN

(Southeast)

A sport to hunt, a feast to enjoy! This bird was brought from West Africa to American shores long before the Declaration of Independence was thought of.

1 3 to 4 pound guinea hen, cleaned (reserve giblets)
2 teaspoons salt
2-1/2 tablespoons butter or margarine
freshly ground pepper
1 teaspoon paprika
1 teaspoon garlic powder
6 strips bacon (uncooked)
1-1/2 cups cooked wild rice, flavored with thyme

Cook giblets, in water to cover, in a saucepan over moderate heat for 10 minutes. Reserve. Preheat oven to 400 degrees. Prepare hen by salting cavity with half the salt and applying remaining half to skin. Rub skin with butter, pepper, paprika, and garlic powder. Since guinea hen might otherwise be dry, place strips of bacon over bird. Mix cooked wild rice flavored with thyme and chopped cooked giblets. Stuff the bird with this mixture. Truss and roast for 50 minutes, or until hen is done. Use a thermometer as for chicken or test for doneness by moving legs. When skin is crisp and legs are easy to move, hen is done.

Serves 4 to 6

BAKED CHICKEN AND OLIVES

(Southwest)

1 3-1/2 pound chicken, cut into serving pieces
3/4 cup flour
1 teaspoon salt
1 tablespoon paprika
1/2 teaspoon garlic powder
1 teaspoon onion powder
1 cup pitted black olives
1 cup orange juice
1 tablespoon honey
2-1/2 cups cooked hot rice

Brown chicken pieces on all sides in a lightly greased skillet over moderate heat. Preheat oven to 375 degrees. Place browned chicken in a square baking dish. In a mixing bowl, combine flour with all remaining ingredients except rice. When thoroughly blended and flour is no longer lumpy, pour sauce over chicken. Bake 1-1/2 hours, or until chicken is fork tender. During baking be sure to baste at least 3 times. Serve with mounds of hot rice.

Serves 6

Relishes

Relishes were an important part of Colonial meals. It is a pity that too few relishes are enjoyed, as they not only add a zestful accompaniment to the meal, but somehow make the main entree seem more flavorsome. A relish, although sometimes used as a salad substitute, is not necessarily such, and for the sake of nutrition a green salad should be included in your meal menu.

JERUSALEM ARTICHOKE RELISH

(South Carolina)

1 pound Jerusalem artichokes
1 cup milk

1 teaspoon salt
1 large green pepper, minced
2 medium onions, minced
1 cup apple cider vinegar
1 cup brown sugar
1 teaspoon mustard powder
juice of 1/2 lemon

Clean artichokes well; do not peel. Place in a deep saucepan with milk and add sufficient water to cover. Add salt, cover, and cook over moderate heat for about 45 minutes, or until tender. Remove and chop well.

In a mixing bowl, combine Jerusalem artichokes, green pepper, and onions. Stir in vinegar and brown sugar. Add mustard powder and lemon juice, and mix well. Allow to stand in mixing bowl at room temperature for 1 hour. Refrigerate.

Serves 4 to 6

PICKLED WATERMELON

(Southern)

Enjoy eating your watermelon, then pickle the rind.

4 quarts water
1-1/2 cups salt
rind of 1 watermelon, cubed
4 pounds brown sugar
1 pint vinegar
1 cup water
1 lemon (including rind) sliced very thin
2 cups raisins
1 teaspoon powdered cloves
2 tablespoons allspice
2 tablespoons cinnamon

Boil water with salt in a deep saucepan. Reduce heat and add watermelon rind. After 10 minutes, remove from stove and allow to stand overnight. In the morning, discard water and replace with clear cool water. Cover and cook over low heat for 1 hour, without allowing water to reach a boil. Again discard water and replace. Cook brown sugar, vinegar, and 1 cup water in a separate saucepan over low heat. Add lemons, raisins, and seasonings. Add melon rind cubes (without water in which it has been soaking) and simmer all ingredients for 1 hour over low heat. Allow to cool at room temperature, then refrigerate in covered containers. An excellent relish to serve with meats and poultry.

Yields about 2-1/2 quarts

LEMON RELISH

(Illinois)

2 large lemons, peeled, seeded, and cut into quarters
1 heaping tablespoon grated lemon rind
1 large onion, minced
1 medium green pepper, finely chopped
1-1/2 cups diced celery
1/2 teaspoon mustard powder
1/2 cup sugar
dash of hot pepper sauce

In a chopping bowl, chop lemon pulp. Turn into a mixing bowl with grated lemon rind, minced onion, chopped green pepper, and diced celery. Mix ingredients well and stir in mustard powder, sugar, and hot pepper sauce. Refrigerate until chilled.

Yields about 1-3/4 cups

CORN RELISH

(Nebraska)

2 cups canned corn niblets, drained
1 cup chopped celery
1 small onion, minced
1 teaspoon prepared mustard
1 teaspoon Worcestershire sauce
2 tablespoons vinegar

Combine all ingredients in a mixing bowl. Cover bowl with plastic wrap, sealing all edges. Refrigerate for 6 hours. Serve with fish.

Serves 4 to 6

PEACH CHUTNEY

(Virginia)

2 pounds peaches, peeled, pitted, and chopped
1 small onion, minced
1/2 cup raisins
1-1/2 cups apple cider vinegar
1 teaspoon garlic powder
1/2 teaspoon salt
1 teaspoon powdered ginger
1-1/4 cups brown sugar
2 tablespoons honey
1 tablespoon mustard seed
1/3 cup halved walnuts

Place peaches, onion, and raisins in a saucepan. Add vinegar and simmer. Season with garlic, salt, and ginger. Stir in brown sugar, then stir in honey. Add mustard seed and walnuts. Cook about 1-1/4 hours until mixture thickens. Stir occasionally to prevent burning. This chutney may be poured into sterilized preserve jars if desired, or it can be eaten when fresh.

Yields about 2-1/2 cups

CRANBERRY RELISH

(Cape Cod)

1 pound cranberries, washed and stemmed
1-1/2 cups crushed fresh pineapple
1/2 cup orange juice
1-1/2 cups granulated sugar

Combine cranberries, pineapple, orange juice, and sugar in a deep saucepan and place over moderate heat. Stir constantly until boiling point is reached and cover. After 5 minutes, skim any foam that may have formed. Uncover pot and continue cooking over slightly lowered heat for 20 minutes, or until fruit should be tender. Turn into bowl, cover with plastic wrap, sealing edges, and refrigerate. This is an excellent meal accompaniment, whether the main course is meat, fish, or fowl.

Yields about 3 cups

APPLE RELISH

(Connecticut)

3-1/2 pounds tart apples, pared and chopped
1-1/2 pounds white onions, minced
1-1/2 cups brown sugar
1 tablespoon salt
1 teaspoon ginger
1 teaspoon mace
1/2 teaspoon powdered cloves
1/4 cup raisins
1-1/4 cups vinegar

Place all ingredients in a deep saucepan. Cover and cook over moderate heat until mixture starts to boil. Reduce heat and simmer for 40 minutes. This relish is equally excellent with fish and meat. Extra amounts may be stored in sealed containers in the refrigerator.

Yields about 1 quart

MARINATED CHICK PEAS

(Southern)

1 pound canned chick peas, drained
1/2 small onion, minced
2 tablespoons pimento, chopped
1/2 cup chopped celery
1/2 teaspoon salt
freshly ground pepper
2 tablespoons wine vinegar
1/4 cup corn oil

Combine all ingredients in a mixing bowl and mix thoroughly Cover bowl with plastic wrap, sealing all edges. Allow to chill in refrigerator for at least 6 hours. This is a tasty delight when served with a fish dish.

Serves 6 to 8

SAUERKRAUT RELISH

(Pennsylvania)

1 pound sauerkraut
1/2 cup granulated brown sugar
1/2 cup chopped celery
1/2 cup chopped raw carrot
freshly ground pepper
1 teaspoon onion powder
1/2 teaspoon garlic powder

Combine all ingredients in a large mixing bowl and stir well. Cover bowl with plastic wrap, sealing all edges, and refrigerate for 24 hours. Serve with a meat and garner your compliments.

Serves 6 to 8

OLD FASHIONED RAISIN RELISH

(Michigan)

2 cups dark seedless raisins
1 teaspoon cinnamon
1/2 teaspoon nutmeg
1 onion, minced
2-1/2 tablespoons tomato catsup
3 tablespoons apple cider vinegar
1 teaspoon sugar

Combine all ingredients in a mixing bowl. Cover bowl with plastic wrap, sealing all edges. Refrigerate for 6 hours. A fine accompaniment with a roasted bird.

Serves 4 to 6

Salads

TOSSED GREENS AND BEANS

(California)

In California, the salad is usually served *before* the main course, and the salads are usually huge.

1/2 head iceberg lettuce, broken into pieces
1 head romaine lettuce, broken into pieces
1/2 teaspoon anchovy paste
1/2 cup canned kidney beans, drained
1/2 cup canned lima beans, drained
1 small onion, chopped
1 large tomato, cut into pieces

DRESSING

6 tablespoons oil

1/4 teaspoon mustard powder
1/4 teaspoon garlic powder
juice of 1 lemon
1 tablespoon wine vinegar
1/4 teaspoon sugar

Toss all salad ingredients in a salad bowl, mix well, and refrigerate. In a separate bowl, blend all dressing ingredients and stir well. Just before serving time, pour dressing over salad and mix thoroughly.

Serves 4 to 6

BEAN SALAD

(Pennsylvania Dutch)

1/2 pound green beans, cooked until barely tender
1/2 pound wax beans, cooked until barely tender
1 cup lima beans, cooked until barely tender
1 medium onion, minced
1/4 cup vinegar
1/2 teaspoon mustard seed

Combine all ingredients in a salad bowl and toss well. Refrigerate and serve as is—no other dressing is needed.

Serves 4 to 6

BEAN SALAD

(Midwest, Shaker)

2 cups green beans, cooked until barely tender
2 cups lettuce, broken into small pieces
1 onion, coarsely chopped
1 tablespoon chopped parsley

Toss all ingredients in a salad bowl. Refrigerate and serve with French dressing or mayonnaise.

Serves 4 to 6

BEET SALAD

(Midwest)

4 fresh medium beets, washed
1/3 cup vinegar
1/2 teaspoon caraway seeds
1/2 teaspoon anise
1 teaspoon sugar
1 tablespoon lemon juice
1/2 cup water
1 tablespoon corn oil

In a saucepan over moderate heat, boil beets in water to cover for about 15 minutes, or until tender. Remove beets and discard water. Holding each beet in turn with a fork, pare and, on a board, cut into thin slices. Return beets to saucepan (drained of cooking water) and add all other ingredients. Cook over low heat for 5 minutes. Allow to cool for 10 minutes at room temperature. Place mixture in a bowl, cover with plastic wrap, sealing all edges, and refrigerate for at least 5 hours. When ready to serve, mix through corn oil.

Serves 6

SPINACH SALAD

(California)

1 package (10 ounces) fresh spinach
1 medium cucumber, thinly sliced
1 medium onion, thinly sliced and separated into rings
1/3 cup corn oil
2-1/2 tablespoons tarragon vinegar
1/2 teaspoon basil
1/2 teaspoon garlic powder
1 teaspoon chopped parsley

Rinse spinach well and break leaves into pieces. Combine with cucumber slices and onion rings in a large salad bowl. In a small bowl, combine corn oil with tarragon vinegar, and season with basil and garlic powder. Add chopped parsley and mix well. Pour oil and vinegar dressing over spinach salad and toss.

Serves 6

OKRA SALAD

(Southeast)

1 10-ounce can okra, or 1 box frozen okra
1 large tomato, cut into eights
1/2 cup celery, diced
1/2 teaspoon mustard seed
1 teaspoon tomato juice
1 medium onion, thinly sliced and separated into rings

Drain liquid from canned okra, or prepare and cook frozen okra according to package directions. Place okra in a salad bowl with tomato, celery, and mustard seeds, and mix thoroughly. Moisten with tomato juice, then spread onion rings on top. Use dressing of your choice. This is an excellent salad with fish.

Serves 4

CAESAR SALAD

(California)

It couldn't have been named for Julius Caesar because it's a native California recipe. In this far Western state, salad is customarily consumed as a first course to the meal.

1 clove garlic, peeled, with 1 piece sliced, remainder minced
1 cup olive oil
1 cup dry bread cubes
1 small head romaine lettuce, washed, dried, and broken
3/4 teaspoon salt
freshly ground pepper
6 anchovy fillets, cut into small pieces
1 (raw) egg
2 tablespoons wine vinegar

Rub salad bowl with slice of garlic. Pour olive oil over bread cubes and sauté in skillet over low heat until the cubes are browned. Mix in bowl with lettuce and season with salt, pepper, and remainder of garlic. Toss and add anchovy fillets. Break egg into mixture and continue vigorous tossing. Sprinkle over wine vinegar and toss once again lightly.

Serves 4 to 6

PICKLED CUCUMBERS

(Hawaii)

2 large cucumbers
handful mustard seeds
1/4 cup vinegar
2 tablespoons sugar
1 tablespoon water
1/4 teaspoon ginger
2 scallions, chopped

Wash cucumbers and slice them paper thin. Place the slices in a deep bowl, add all other ingredients, and stir well. Allow to stand at room temperature for at least 1/2 hour before refrigerating.

Serves 4 to 6

APPLE-CABBAGE SLAW

(New York)

1 small head cabbage, shredded
1 large red apple (any variety) washed, cored, and minced
3 tablespoons apple cider vinegar
1-1/2 tablespoons mayonnaise
2 tablespoons chopped walnuts (unsalted)

Shred cabbage into a mixing bowl, add minced apple, and mix well. Pour apple cider vinegar over ingredients and toss. Allow to stand for 30 minutes, then mix through mayonnaise. (Do not increase the amount of mayonnaise. For best slaw, mayonnaise should always be scant.) Sprinkle chopped walnuts over all.

Serves 6

LATE SUMMER COLESLAW

(Northeast)

1 medium cabbage
2 tablespoons vinegar
1/4 cup mayonnaise
handful mustard seeds

Using a sharp knife, slice the cabbage into shreds. Pour vinegar over shredded cabbage and mix well. Allow to stand for 30 minutes. Add mayonnaise, mix well, and work mustard seeds through. Refrigerate and serve.

Serves 4 to 6

FRUITED CHICKEN SALAD

(Western)

3 cups diced chicken
3/4 cup diced celery
1 cup orange segments, pitted
1 cup pineapple chunks, fresh or canned
1/4 cup slivered almonds
1/4 cup orange juice
1/3 cup mayonnaise
1 teaspoon salt
freshly ground pepper
1 tablespoon paprika

Combine chicken, celery, orange, pineapple, and almonds in a salad bowl. In a small mixing bowl, combine orange juice, mayonnaise, salt, pepper, and paprika. Add to chicken mixture and blend well so as to coat all ingredients. If your preference is for a more moist dressing, add a little more mayonnaise, or 2 or 3 tablespoons commercial French dressing.

Serves 6 to 8

AVOCADO FRUIT SALAD

(California)

1 head crisp lettuce
2 cups grapefruit segments
2 medium avocados, peeled and thinly sliced
1 cup seedless grapes
1/2 cup walnuts, chopped
1/4 cup grapefruit juice
1/3 cup mayonnaise.
paprika

Wash and break lettuce leaves, and arrange on 4 individual salad plates. In a mixing bowl, combine grapefruit segments, avocado slices, grapes, and walnuts. Toss to mix well, but do so gently so as not to injure fruit. In a separate bowl, combine grapefruit juice and mayonnaise, blend well, and add paprika. Arrange fruit on lettuce and pour dressing over fruit.

Serves 4

RICE SALAD

(Southern)

1 cup cooked rice, refrigerated until cool
1 medium onion, minced
1 medium green pepper, minced
1/2 cup diced celery
1 tomato, diced
1 teaspoon salt
freshly ground pepper
1 teaspoon basil
1/4 cup commercial French dressing
1 small head chicory (sometimes called endive in the South)

Combine all ingredients except chicory in a salad bowl. Wash chicory well, break in pieces, and pile salad atop chicory.

Serves 4 to 6

WALDORF SALAD

(New York City)

Devised by and named for the famous hotel, this is a fine salad to accompany a light meal.

4 medium apples, peeled and diced
1 cup diced celery
1 tablespoon lemon juice
1/3 cup mayonnaise
1/4 cup walnuts, chopped
lettuce

In a mixing bowl, blend apples and celery, sprinkle on lemon juice, and mix thoroughly. Add mayonnaise and mix well. Add walnuts and mix them into the other ingredients.

Serve on lettuce leaves fashioned into cups.

Serves 4 to 6

Sauces and Dips

PORTLAND STEAK SAUCE

(Oregon)

1 cup water
1-1/2 tablespoons vinegar
1/2 teaspoon onion powder
2 egg yolks, lightly beaten
2 tablespoons butter or margarine
1 tablespoon Worcestershire sauce
1 teaspoon lemon juice
1/2 teaspoon prepared mustard

Combine water and vinegar in a saucepan over low heat. Add onion powder and gradually stir in beaten egg yolks. Continue stirring and add butter or margarine, then Worcestershire sauce, lemon juice, and prepared mustard. When fully heated (before boiling point is reached), pour over any cut of broiled steak.

RAISIN SPICE SAUCE

(Southwest)

Here is a sauce that imparts fresh flavor to a plain meat or leftovers.

2 tablespoons butter or margarine
1 small onion, chopped
1/4 cup chopped green pepper
1 teaspoon garlic powder
1-1/2 teaspoons chili powder
1 teaspoon sugar
1/2 teaspoon salt
dash of hot pepper sauce
1 tablespoon sherry
1 cup tomato sauce
1 cup beef bouillon
2/3 cup dark raisins

In a heavy saucepan over low heat, melt butter or margarine and add each ingredient in sequence, working quickly. Stir once in a while and simmer for 12 minutes. This may be served immediately, but can also be tightly covered and stored in the refrigerator. If the sauce has been stored, heat sauce before spooning over meat as a sauce or in place of gravy.

Yields about 2 cups

BARBECUE SAUCE

(Georgia)

1 tablespoon salt
1 tablespoon sugar
1 tablespoon dry mustard
1 tablespoon celery salt
1 tablespoon hot pepper sauce
freshly ground pepper
2 tablespoons paprika
2 tablespoons cornstarch
1/2 teaspoon allspice
1/2 teaspoon cloves
1 tablespoon onion powder
1 quart tomato juice
1 cup vinegar

Mix the dry ingredients in a saucepan. Add tomato juice and simmer over low heat for 30 minutes. Gradually stir in vinegar and continue simmering for 10 minutes more. This sauce may be made in quantity and stores in tightly closed containers in the refrigerator. Brush steak on all sides with this, particularly if grilling outdoors.

Yields about 1-1/4 quarts

GUACAMOLE

(Southwest)

The avocado, like corn, is a native plant, and its cultivation is another of the agricultural gifts of the red-skinned peoples of the Southwest. Probably the most renowned recipe involving avocado is the following, which is enjoyed as an appetizer dip, although in the Southwest it is often thinned and used as a sauce for other foods.

2 ripe avocados
1 small onion, grated
juice of 1/2 lemon
1/4 teaspoon garlic powder
1/2 teaspoon Worcestershire sauce
1 tablespoon chili sauce
1/8 teaspoon salt
1 tablespoon mayonnaise

Peel, pit (retain the pit), and mash avocado flesh in a mixing bowl, working with a fork to better break the flesh down. Mix in onion and lemon juice and, using a mixing spoon, stir in garlic powder, Worcestershire sauce, chili sauce, salt, and mayonnaise. When mixture is completely smooth, place in the refrigerator until ready for use. Place the avocado pit into the mixture while it is being refrigerated, so that the guacamole will not blacken. Remove pit before serving. If you wish, ring the dip with corn crackers.

Makes 2-1/2 cups

Vegetables

ARTICHOKES

(Eastern)

4 artichokes (select heavy ones, with thick green leaves folded tightly to give the artichoke a full shape)
1 teaspoon salt
1 tablespoon cooking oil
juice of 1 lemon
1/4 teaspoon garlic powder

Place artichokes upright in a deep saucepan and add water to a depth of 1 inch. (Try to arrange artichokes in a saucepan of a size to keep them upright during cooking.) Season with salt, oil, lemon juice, and garlic. Cover and, over moderate heat, allow to reach a boil. Lower heat a bit and continue to boil for 30 to 40 minutes, depending upon the size of the artichokes.

(A large size requires longer cooking than a smaller size.) They are done when the stem is fork tender. Remove artichokes from the pot with kitchen tongs, or by using two tablespoons like a vise. Allow to drain upside down.

Serve hot, with leaves upright, as a separate course following the main course.

HOT BUTTER SAUCE

1/4 pound melted butter
juice of 1/2 lemon
dash of paprika

Mix all ingredients and bring to the table in a little bowl. Eat artichoke by pulling off leaves with fingers, one at a time, dipping each in sauce, and scraping away the soft part with the teeth. Do not eat the fibrous choke, but remove it with knife and fork. Under this is the heart. Cut this into pieces and eat with your fork, dipping it into the sauce at will.

Serves 4

ARTICHOKES

(Western)

4 artichokes (select heavy ones, with thick green leaves folded tightly to give the artichoke a full shape)
1 tablespoon oil
2 cloves of garlic (whole)
1 lemon, sliced
2 teaspoons salt

Place artichokes in a Dutch oven and cover them with water. Add all other ingredients and place a heavy plate that will not be affected by heat across the artichokes. Cover and boil over high heat for 25 to 40 minutes, or until stems are fork tender. Remove from heat and drain artichokes with leaves facing down. Refrigerate.

COLD DRESSING

1/3 cup mayonnaise
juice of 1/2 lemon
dash of mustard powder

Mix all ingredients well and serve in a bowl. Serve artichokes cold in upright position and eat as described in previous recipe (Artichokes —Eastern).

Serves 4

ASPARAGUS

(Iowa)

1-1/2 pounds fresh asparagus
1 teaspoon salt
1/4 cup melted butter
juice of 1/2 lemon

Cut tough ends off asparagus and wash under running water, gently brushing to dislodge all grit and dirt. Place lengthwise in a saucepan large enough to accommodate spears, one layer on another, if necessary. Fill pan with 1-1/2 inches of water and add salt. Cover and cook over moderate neat until boiling and then allow to boil for 3 minutes. Reduce heat immediately and simmer for 10 minutes. Drain water and serve hot. Pour melted butter and lemon juice over asparagus.

Serves 4

BAKED ASPARAGUS

(Nebraska)

1-1/2 pounds cooked asparagus spears (see preceding recipe)
3/4 cup cheddar cheese, grated
1/4 cup Swiss cheese, slivered
3/4 teaspoon salt
freshly ground pepper
1/4 cup chicken broth
1/4 cup heavy cream
2-1/2 tablespoons flour
4 tablespoons butter or margarine
paprika

Preheat oven to 375 degrees. Place cooked asparagus in a greased, oblong baking dish. Combine cheddar cheese, Swiss cheese, salt, pepper, chicken broth, cream, and flour in a mixing bowl or electric blender. Blend well and pour over asparagus. Dot with butter or margarine and sprinkle on paprika. Bake for 15 minutes.

Serves 4

PERFECTION RICE

(North and South Carolina)

Thomas Jefferson was not only a man of patriotism and politics, he was superbly talented in architecture. Witness the enduring perfection of Monticello, his renowned home. In his home, his guests partook of marvelous meals that were not the general custom of the day. He had an abiding interest in agriculture and animal husbandry, and what he could not otherwise grow or breed he imported, even smuggling grains of rice concealed in his pockets—this at a time when illegal transportation of rice carried a death penalty. This is said to be the origin of the famed long-grain Carolina-grown rice.

1 cup long-grain rice
1-1/2 cups water (cool)
1/4 teaspoon salt
1 teaspoon lemon juice
1 tablespoon butter or margarine

Place rice and water in a deep saucepan. Add salt and lemon juice, and cook uncovered over moderate heat until water boils. Then lower heat and stir once with a fork while adding butter. Simmer uncovered for about 17 minutes more, or until water has been entirely absorbed and rice is dry and not sticky. (Should a bit more water be required during cooking, use your judgment in adding just a little.) When done, remove rice from heat, shake pot once, and serve as a vegetable on its own, or as part of another recipe.

Serves 4

ROASTED CORN

(Arizona)

1/4 pound softened, sweet butter
1/2 teaspoon onion powder
1 teaspoon salt
6 ears corn, with husks

In a bowl, combine butter, onion powder, and salt and reserve.

Without detaching husks, carefully open and remove cornsilk. Brush butter mixture over kernels and seal husks about corn again, holding shut with a tied thread at end, if needed, to prevent husk opening during roasting.

Preheat oven to 375 degrees. Place ears in lightly greased roasting pan. Bake for 30 minutes, turning ears occasionally. Cut any threads off and serve in husks to allow corn to self-steam on plates until opened for eating.

Serves 6

SAUERKRAUT

(Pennsylvania Dutch)

George Washington, while on hard winter campaign, had a Pennsylvania Dutch cook. He and the soldiers who survived Valley Forge brought to their home colonies a taste for Pennsylvania cooking. George Washington brought back the cook.

Sauerkraut has been prominent on Pennsylvania Dutch menus since Colonial days. It is considered a promise of good health and good fortune to consume a helping of sauerkraut on New Year's Day. Be warned making sauerkraut yourself requires much patience.

1 4-pound firm cabbage
1-3/4 tablespoons salt

Tear off outer cabbage leaves, which may be blemished or tough, and wash these and reserve. Shred the remainder of the cabbage head into a large bowl, and thoroughly mix the salt through.

Spoon into a stone crock of sufficient size to hold contents enough cabbage to cover the bottom. Press down on cabbage with a potato masher, using some strength in doing so. Brine will rise as you apply pressure. Repeat procedure, layer by layer, until all of the cabbage is used. Place a layer of outer leaves on top, and add a plate on top of the leaves with a weight on the plate. Fasten muslin tightly across the top of the crock.

Two or three times a week, remove the cloth and replace with a clean one. Wash the plate and the inner walls of the crock, and retie with clean muslin. If you wish, you may launder the old cloth for use again. In three weeks, the sauerkraut will be ready for use.

Serves 12

SPICED BUTTERNUT SQUASH

(New Hampshire)

2 butternut squash, cut into halves, with seeds removed
1/4 cup butter or margarine
1/2 teaspoon allspice
1 teaspoon ground ginger
2 tablespoons maple syrup

Preheat oven to 350 degrees. Dot cut side with dabs of butter or margarine, sprinkle over allspice and ginger, and spoon over maple syrup. Bake cut side up for 1 hour or until squash flesh is of the consistency of baked sweet potato. If required, return to oven for 10 minutes more.

Serves 4

SOY VEGETABLE CASSEROLE

(San Francisco)

The Chinese were originally imported as laborers for the building of railroad lines. They chiefly settled in San Francisco, and many who had the knowledge of delicate Chinese cuisine became chefs.

1/2 cup water chestnuts, chopped
2 medium onions, chopped
1/4 cup celery, chopped
1 cup bean sprouts, chopped
1/2 cup cauliflower, chopped
2 eggs, lightly beaten
2 tablespoons sherry
1/4 cup soy sauce
1/4 pound butter

Preheat oven to 325 degrees. In a mixing bowl, blend water chestnuts, onions, celery, bean sprouts, and cauliflower. Mix through beaten eggs, season with sherry and soy sauce, and blend all ingredients well. Turn into greased 1-quart casserole and dot with butter. Bake for 45 minutes.

Serves 4

BOSTON BAKED BEANS

(Boston)

1 pound dried navy beans
1 teaspoon salt
1 tablespoon mustard powder
1/3 cup molasses
1/2 cup brown sugar
1 medium onion, minced
1/2 pound salt pork, cut into pieces
3/4 teaspoon powdered cloves
1-1/2 cups ketchup
4 strips bacon

Wash beans, cover with cold water, and soak overnight at room temperature. Place drained beans in an earthenware bean pot or a Dutch oven with a little of the water (about 2 inches deep). Cover and simmer for 1 hour. Preheat oven to 275 degrees. Turn beans into a greased casserole and add salt, mustard, molasses, brown sugar, onion, salt pork, cloves, and ketchup. Mix all ingredients well and place bacon strips on top. Cover and bake for about 5 hours and 50 minutes. Remove cover and cook for 40 minutes more.

Serves 6 to 8

ROUNDUP BEANS

(Oregon)

1/2 pound kidney beans
1/2 pound pea beans
1 large onion, chopped
1-1/4 teaspoons salt
freshly ground pepper
3/4 cup brown sugar
1-1/2 cups ketchup
1 teaspoon mustard powder
1 pound bacon

Wash beans and soak overnight in water to cover. Drain beans and turn into a greased crock or casserole. Preheat oven to 300 degrees. Mix onion, salt, pepper, brown sugar, ketchup, and mustard powder through the beans. Place bacon on top. Cover and bake for 6 hours. If needed, add a little boiling water from time to time to keep beans moist.

Serves 6 to 8

BARBECUE BEAN CASSEROLE

(Texas)

1 pound red kidney beans
1 1-pound can tomatoes and liquid
1-1/4 cups mashed potatoes
2 medium onions, chopped
1 green pepper, chopped
1 teaspoon salt
freshly ground pepper
1 teaspoon Worcestershire sauce
8 bacon strips, fried and crumbled

Wash and, in a deep saucepan, soak beans in water to cover for 1 hour. Then place over moderate heat and allow to reach a boil. Lower heat and simmer for 2-1/2 hours. Preheat oven to 375 degrees. Drain beans, place in a greased 1-1/2 quart casserole, add tomatoes with their liquid, mashed potatoes, onions, green pepper, salt, pepper, Worcestershire sauce, and mix all ingredients well. Sprinkle bacon crumbs over all. Bake for 35 minutes.

Serves 6 to 8

BLACK-EYED PEAS

(Southeast)

1 pound dried black-eyed peas
2 medium onions, chopped coarsely
3 strips bacon, fried and crumbled
1 teaspoon salt
dash of hot pepper sauce

Wash peas in cold running water. Place in a saucepan and fill with water to within 1/4 from the rim of the pot. Allow peas to soak at room temperature for at least 4 hours. Place pot over moderate heat and cook until water begins to boil. Immediately lower heat and simmer for 2-1/4 hours, or until peas are tender. Pour off all but 1/2 cup water and quickly add onions, bacon, salt, and pepper sauce. Cover pot and simmer for 10 minutes, stirring ingredients once during cooking. The onions, which are half-cooked, and the soft peas form an interesting combination of textures.

Serves 6

PILAU

(Southeast)

2 cups cooked tomatoes
2 stalks celery, chopped
1 medium onion, minced
1 cup frozen peas
1/2 cup canned or frozen okra, sliced
1 cup uncooked rice
1 teaspoon salt
freshly ground pepper
1 teaspoon sugar
dash of hot pepper sauce
1-1/2 tablespoons butter
1 pint boiling water
1 pound cooked meat cut into bite-size pieces, or seafood (your choice)

Heat tomatoes in a deep saucepan over moderate heat and add celery, onion, frozen peas, okra, and rice. Season with salt, pepper, and sugar. Quickly add hot pepper sauce and butter. Pour boiling water over all and mix ingredients well. Bring liquid to a boil in the saucepan, then immediately reduce heat to a simmer. Cover and cook for 40 minutes. Add cooked meat or seafood and stir well. Serve with a crisp salad.

Serves 4

SWEET-SOUR CABBAGE

(Pennsylvania Dutch)

1 medium cabbage, cut into wide shreds
1 medium onion, minced
bacon drippings
1/4 cup brown sugar
1/3 cup vinegar
1 tablespoon lemon juice
2-1/2 tablespoons flour
1/2 teaspoon salt
freshly ground pepper
6 slices bacon, fried and crumbled

Cover shredded cabbage with water and cook in a saucepan over moderate heat for 8 to 10 minutes, or until tender. Drain and set aside.

In a skillet over low heat, sauté onion in bacon drippings. Add brown sugar, vinegar, lemon juice, flour, salt, and pepper. Stir constantly and add more flour if needed to sufficiently thicken. Place cabbage in a bowl and pour sauce over. Sprinkle bacon crumbs over all.

Serves 4 to 6

MAPLE CARROTS

(Vermont)

1-1/4 pounds fresh carrots, with tops cut off
1 teaspoon sugar
1/2 teaspoon salt

Scrape whole carrots, place in a saucepan large enough to accommodate them, and add sugar and salt. Add about 1 inch of water and cook over moderate heat. Allow to come to a boil and continue to boil for 15 minutes.

1/3 cup maple syrup
2 tablespoons orange juice
3 tablespoons butter or margarine

Drain carrots, pour maple syrup and orange juice over them, and add butter or margarine. Simmer just long enough to melt the butter. Serve carrots whole or halved.

Serves 4

GLAZED CARROTS

(Indiana)

1 tablespoon plus 1 teaspoon butter or margarine
12 small carrots, cut into 1-inch lengths
1/2 teaspoon salt
1/4 cup maple syrup
1 teaspoon grated orange rind
1 tablespoon brown sugar
1/2 teaspoon nutmeg

Melt butter or margarine in a saucepan over low heat and add carrots. Season with salt and add about 1-1/2 inches of water to the pot. Cover and simmer for 12 minutes, or until carrots are just a little crisper than tender. Pour over maple syrup and sprinkle on orange rind, brown sugar, and nutmeg. Continue to simmer uncovered for 4 minutes more. This is a delicious contrast of sweet flavor for the main course.

Serves 4 to 6

SCALLOPED CORN

(Southwest)

1 1-pound can creamed corn
2 eggs, lightly beaten
1 cup light cream
1/2 cup bread crumbs
2 tablespoons sugar
3/4 teaspoon salt
freshly ground pepper
1-1/2 teaspoons Worcestershire sauce
1-1/2 tablespoons green chili peppers, chopped
3/4 cup sharp cheddar cheese, grated

Preheat oven to 375 degrees. Combine all ingredients except chili peppers and cheddar cheese in a mixing bowl. In a separate bowl, combine chili and cheese. Turn corn mixture into a greased 1-quart casserole and spread cheese mixture on top. Bake for 30 minutes. Lower heat to 325 degrees and bake for 35 minutes more.

Serves 6

CORN ON THE COB

(Midwest)

In the Corn Belt of the United States, for miles on end, row upon row of corn is planted. Once an Indian staple, corn has become an important crop for all of America. Nothing can compare with freshly picked and husked corn. If, like most urban Americans, your home isn't close to a farm, you have to do the best you are able to in the vegetable market. Test corn for freshness by piercing a kernel with your fingernail. If it spits a milky liquid back at you, it is fresh. Then hurry it into the pot.

4 ears of corn
1 tablespoon milk
2 teaspoons sugar
boiling water to cover

Place sufficient water in a large kettle to cover the husked ears of corn (or to give them enough floating room). Save one outer husk to place in the water. Allow water to come to a full boil, add milk and sugar, and insert the corn. Keep uncovered and, when water reaches a new boil, cook for 3-1/2 minutes longer. Remove at once. Drain and eat hot, with butter.

Serves 4

SKILLET CORN

(Northwest)

5 tablespoons butter or margarine
kernels from 5 or 6 medium to large corn cobs
1 small onion, minced
1/2 cup canned tomatoes
1/4 teaspoon garlic powder
1 teaspoon salt
freshly ground pepper
1/3 cup cheddar cheese, grated

This is a good way to use corn that may not be farm fresh. Melt butter or margarine in a skillet over low heat. Add corn kernels, onion, tomatoes, garlic, salt, and pepper. Cover and cook for 15 minutes. Add cheddar cheese and butter and mix well. Cook uncovered for 3 to 4 more minutes.

Serves 4 to 6

MARIGOLD RICE

(Southern)

2-1/4 cups chicken broth
2 cups instant rice
1 medium onion, chopped coarsely, and sautéed prior to use
1/8 teaspoon salt
2-1/2 teaspoon dried marigold petals

Heat chicken broth in a saucepan over moderate heat until boiling. Remove from heat and quickly spoon in rice, onion, salt, and marigold petals. Allow to stand for about 17 minutes with the pot covered. Stir once after 5 minutes, then recover. Do not remove cover for remainder of standing time. Liquid should then be fully absorbed.

Serves 4 to 5

SPICED GLAZED PARSNIPS

(Southeast)

6 medium parsnips, washed and quartered
2-1/2 tablespoons butter or margarine
1/4 cup brown sugar, firmly packed
1/4 teaspoon salt
1/4 cup apple cider vinegar
2-1/2 tablespoons orange juice

Cook unpared parsnips, with salted water to cover, in a covered saucepan over moderate heat. Allow to boil for 10 minutes, then reduce heat. Simmer for 30 minutes and test parsnips with a fork for tenderness. Remove skins while hot. Melt butter in a skillet over low heat. Add brown sugar, salt, vinegar, and orange juice. Spoon the liquid over the parsnips and sauté for about 5 minutes, or until parsnips are well glazed. This is an excellent accompaniment with meat.

Serves 4 to 6

BOILED TURNIP GREENS

(Southern)

Although this recipe is a very old one, today it fits the newer classification of *Soul Food.*

pork bone and 1/2 pound pork, cut into small pieces
2 bunches young turnip greens, washed and cut
3 whole turnips, pared and coarsely chopped
1/2 teaspoon salt
2 tablespoons butter or margarine
1/4 cup dry, fine bread crumbs or wheat germ

In a saucepan, place pork bone and meat in water to cover. Add greens and turnips, and season with salt. Simmer over low heat for 45 to 50 minutes. Make sure that water doesn't cook out; add more water if necessary. When greens are tender, turn into serving bowl and dot with butter, then sprinkle crumbs over all. This is a flavorsome substitute for a more usual vegetable.

Serves 4 to 6

MINTED GREEN PEAS

(Virginia)

This recipe, which originated in the kitchens of Jeffersonian Virginia, has survived time. There, families proudly grew and served green beans, and gentlemen placed wagers on the first crop of each year to reach table.

3 cups shelled peas
1/2 cup water
3 tablespoons butter or margarine
1 shallot, chopped (with green top)
1 teaspoon salt
freshly ground pepper
1 tablespoon sugar
2 teaspoons chopped mint

Blend peas, water and butter or margarine in a saucepan over low heat. Cover and simmer for 10 minutes. Add chopped shallot, salt, and pepper. Cover again and simmer for 15 to 20 minutes longer, or until peas are tender. Stir in sugar and chopped mint.

Serves 6 to 8

HOOSIER STUFFED PEPPERS

(Indiana)

4 medium-size sweet peppers, red or green
1/2 teaspoon salt

Cut tops off peppers and, being careful to keep them otherwise intact, remove the seeds and fibers. Place the peppers with water to cover in a saucepan, add salt, and cook over moderate heat for 8 to 10 minutes.

1-1/4 cups rice, cooked according to package instructions
1/4 teaspoon salt
freshly ground pepper
1-1/2 tablespoons heavy cream
2/3 cup stewed tomatoes, canned
1/4 cup parmesan cheese, grated

Preheat oven to 350 degrees. In a bowl, mix cooked rice with salt, pepper, and cream. Stuff pepper shells. Pour tomatoes over all. Dust with parmesan cheese. Bake for 12 to 14 minutes.

Serves 4

STEWED RADISHES WITH TOPS

(Southern)

2 bunches fresh radishes with tops intact
1/2 teaspoon salt
freshly ground pepper
1 tablespoon sugar
1/2 cup milk
1/2 teaspoon nutmeg
1 tablespoon butter or margarine

Prepare radishes by washing well in cold running water. Cut tops away from radishes, and place radishes and tops with water to cover in a saucepan over low heat. Allow to reach boiling point, then simmer for 8 minutes with heat reduced. Season with salt, pepper, and sugar and add milk while stirring well. Serve with meat or fish as an extra vegetable. Spoon a very little of the liquid over the radishes. Dust nutmeg over and place a dab of butter or margarine atop each serving.

Serves 4 or 5

CREAMED RADISHES

(New York, Shaker)

4 tablespoons butter or margarine
2-1/2 tablespoons flour
3/4 teaspoon salt
1/2 teaspoon sage
3/4 cup milk
4 cups radishes, cleaned and sliced, but not scraped
1 small onion minced
3/4 cup heavy cream
freshly ground pepper

Melt butter or margarine in a saucepan over low heat and add flour while stirring well. Season with salt and sage. Gradually stir in milk. Add radishes and onion and, lastly, stir in cream. Heat over low heat until cream is heated. Turn into a serving dish and sprinkle pepper over all. This is quite souplike and, if you wish, the quantities of milk and cream may be cut down.

Serves 4

SARATOGA CHIPS

(Saratoga, New York)

In the late 1800s, an angry chef thought to irritate a complaining diner. When the waiter returned uneaten French fried potatoes to the chef with the customer's complaint, the chef of the old *United States Hotel*, who was far more spirited than his surname of Crum might indicate, sliced paper-thin slabs of potatoes and fried them in deep fat. The diner was unexpectedly delighted, but it was the fashionable watering and racing town, not Chef Crum, that lent its name to the delicacy. Such is the penalty of being born with the wrong name!

4 medium potatoes
fat for deep frying
1 tablespoon salt

Pare potatoes and slice wafer thin. Careful strokes of a knife or a vegetable slicer will achieve this. Place slices in a deep bowl filled with cold water and allow to remain for 1-1/2 hours. Dry slices by spreading on paper toweling, and immerse in heated fat in a skillet with high sides or in a deep fryer. Remove and drain on paper toweling again. Sprinkle salt over all.

Serves 4 to 6

COCONUT MASHED POTATOES

(California)

5 medium potatoes
1 cup coconut milk
2 tablespoons light cream
1/2 teaspoon ginger
1/2 teaspoon sugar

Pare and cut potatoes into pieces, and boil in salted water to cover for 20 minutes, or until potatoes are tender. Drain, mash with potato masher, and gradually work in the coconut milk. When potatoes are well mashed, use a spoon to whip well, add cream, and flavor with ginger and sugar. If necessary, add more coconut milk or cream to lighten consistency. Serve hot.

Serves 6

Fritters and Such

TACOS

(Arizona)

Tacos are popular in Arizona, while enchiladas are favored in New Mexico. Both are often purchased at stands, where they are eaten standing up.

Enchiladas are so closely akin to tacos that even experts disagree as to which is which. The Southwest definition is that enchiladas are baked and tacos are fried. Tacos consist of tortillas wrapped, open-ended, around fillings, usually cheese or meat mixtures or the combination of both.

Enchiladas can be eaten sandwich style, in quintuple stacks, or with the filling in half-folded tortillas. These also are stacked, and often each layer of filling is different.

Prepare tortillas.

BEEF FILLING

1/2 pound chopped beef
2 tablespoons cooking oil
1/2 small onion, minced
1/4 teaspoon garlic powder
1/4 teaspoon chili powder
1/8 teaspoon cumin powder
2-1/2 tablespoons lukewarm water
1 tablespoon cooking oil
1/4 teaspoon salt
freshly ground pepper

Heat oil and blend all ingredients in a skillet over low heat. When meat is browned, spread between halves of folded tortillas.

CHICKEN FILLING

1 boned and skinned breast of cooked chicken, minced
1/2 small onion, minced
1/2 teaspoon chopped chili
1/2 teaspoon coriander
1/2 teaspoon salt
freshly ground pepper
2 tablespoons tomato paste
1 tablespoon cooking oil

Heat oil in a skillet over low flame, add all ingredients, and mix well. When mixture is well blended and heated, spread between folded halves of tortillas.

PORK FILLING

1/2 pound cooked lean pork, minced
2 tablespoons tomato paste
1/4 teaspoon oregano
1/2 teaspoon chopped chili
1/2 small onion, minced
1/2 teaspoon salt
freshly ground pepper
1/4 teaspoon coriander
1 tablespoon cooking oil

Heat oil in a skillet over low heat, add all ingredients, and blend well. When mixture is thoroughly mixed and heated, spread between folded halves of tortillas.

PUFFED CORN OYSTERS

(New Mexico)

Corn is essentially North American, thought to have originated as a hybrid of native grasses, probably in the Southwest. However, a strain of corn may originally have been carried north from the Incas into Mexico, eventually reaching the land that was to become our border states. Indian lore provides more fanciful, intriguing tales of corn's inception. These usually have to do with a spirit figure bestowing it to the soil, and most Indian tribes have some form of ceremony of adulation to corn.

These are all corn, with no oysters!

3 cups corn kernels, fresh, frozen, or canned
3 eggs, separated
1/3 cup all-purpose flour
1/2 teaspoon baking powder
1/2 teaspoon salt
freshly ground pepper
1/4 teaspoon garlic powder

If the corn is fresh, husk and remove corn silk, cut kernels off the cob, and scrape to remove any of the kernels and pulp still adhering to the cob. Place kernels and pulp in a mixing bowl. In a smaller bowl, beat egg yolks until lemony and blend into corn, mixing well. Sift flour, baking powder, salt, pepper, and garlic powder into the corn and mix well. Beat egg whites in a separate bowl until they are stiffly peaked and fold into corn mixture, blending thoroughly.

Grease and heat a griddle or skillet and drop heaping teaspoonfuls of batter onto the surface. The dough will swell and look similar to an oyster. Turn puffs to ensure even browning on all sides. When sufficiently brown (about 4 minutes), remove to paper toweling. Allow to drain and serve hot.

These are excellent as cocktail party fare, a main course, or as an accompaniment to a meat or fish dish.

Yields about 3-1/2 dozen

FLAPJACKS

(Northwest)

It may be that Clementine made these for the miners '49ers, but they originated in logging camps to satisfy hungry men. These are known as griddle cakes, and in Minnesota they were called a *string of flats.*

2 cups all-purpose flour
2 tablespoons baking powder
1 teaspoon salt
2 tablespoons sugar
3 eggs
2 cups milk
1/4 pound butter or margarine

Sift flour, baking powder, salt, and sugar into a mixing bowl. Break eggs into mixture and mix well. Add milk and continue beating. Grease griddle or skillet with butter or margarine and place over moderate heat until hot. Ladle batter onto hot surface. Cook until underside is done, then flap over to brown other side. During cooking, add more butter or margarine to griddle or skillet, as required. Serve in stacks with maple syrup.

Serves 4

SOURDOUGH PANCAKES

(Alaska)

3 cups sourdough spongs (see sourdough recipe)
2 eggs
1/3 cup water
1 teaspoon baking soda
1 teaspoon salt
1-1/2 tablespoons sugar
1 tablespoon oil or melted butter

Thoroughly mix all ingredients in a mixing bowl until the batter is somewhat liquified and frothy. Grease a griddle or skillet with oil or melted butter, heat, and pour on rounds of batter. The under side is brown when bubbles appear on the upper side. Flip over and brown the other side. Serve with your favorite syrup.

Serves 6

SOURDOUGH

(Alaska)

In this harsh, cold country, yeast was not readily obtainable, so prospectors and fur trappers held on to their sourdough starters as their most precious possession. Often a sourdough starter would be tucked into a tin can, its handle fastened to their belts. Sometimes the dough was inherited. Occasionally, it was purchased for cash, skins, or gold. The starters have a life of their own, and the best sourdough starter wads have a history extending several hundred years into the past. Actually, "sour" is a misnomer, as the dough can be mixed into delicious, chiffon-light pancakes that would be the envy of any housewife used to the packaged mixes. Recently, in the delicacies section of a food store, I came upon commercially packaged starters—wads or sponges of dough about the size of a silver dollar and said to be of a line two hundred years old. However, if you want to start a dynasty, why not initiate your own starter? There are only two rules governing the care of it. Maintain it in the refrigerator, and use it regularly on an average of at least once a week. Always use part of the starter sponge and retain part.

1 cup flour
1 cup water
1 package yeast

Place all ingredients in a pint-size glass jar and mix. Allow to remain covered at room temperature overnight.

2 cups warm water
2 cups flour
contents of starter jar

Turn starter into a mixing bowl, add water and flour, and beat until batter is smooth and thin enough to pour. If needed, add a bit more warm water. Keep the bowl in a warm place overnight, so that it will rise. The next morning, remove about 1/3 cup of the sponge. Place this in the washed pint jar. Cover it and keep refrigerated until you wish to make the next sponge. *Note:* It should be used within a week to keep it viable. Otherwise, to extend its potency, add just flour to it. Form the dough into a ball and store in a covered container. To use it later on, merely add a measure of warm water and flour (as used for this sponge).

JOHNNY CAKES

(Rhode Island)

Johnny is a contraction of *journey*. Cakes such as these were the early settlers' snacks to fortify them on their travels from one settlement to another on a day's business.

1 cup cornmeal
1 teaspoon salt
3/4 teaspoon sugar
1 cup milk, scalded

In a bowl, mix corn meal with salt and sugar, and gradually stir in milk. Place tablespoonfuls of batter across the surface of a hot, greased griddle or skillet. When cakes brown on underside, turn with spatula and brown the other side, allowing about 4-1/2 minutes to brown underside and about 3-1/2 minutes for the other.

Serve the cakes like pancakes with maple syrup, or allow to cool and eat as a bread with butter.

Makes about 2 dozen

FLANNEL CAKES

(Southwest)

1-1/2 cups all-purpose flour
2/3 tablespoon baking powder
1 tablespoon sugar
1/2 teaspoon salt
1 eggs
1-1/4 cups milk
3 tablespoons butter or margarine

Sift flour, baking powder, sugar, and salt into a mixing bowl. Break in egg, pour in milk, and beat thoroughly until all ingredients are well blended and there are no lumps in the batter. Melt butter or margarine in a skillet over low heat. Gradually increase heat slightly, being careful that butter doesn't smoke or turn brown. Drop into skillet enough batter to spread to about 4 inches. Do not allow cakes to touch. Cook for about 1-1/4 minutes, or until underside is brown. Underside is brown when bubbles form in the batter. Brown other side for about 1/2 minute. Serve in stacks of about 4 cakes.

Serves 4

HUSH PUPPIES

(Texas)

Would you believe that they used to throw these to the hounds to keep them quiet while the humans ate?

1 cup cornmeal
1 teaspoon baking powder
1/2 teaspoon salt
2 tablespoons minced onion
3/4 cup milk
cooking oil

Combine cornmeal, baking powder, and salt in a mixing bowl. Blend thoroughly, add minced onion, and gradually stir in milk.

Pour cooking oil to a depth of 1-1/4 inches in the skillet and heat over a low flame. Dip a tablespoon into the oil and then into the cornmeal batter. With your fingers, shape each spoonful into a flat, round cake. Drop into heated oil, cook 3 to 4 minutes until brown, and remove to drain on paper toweling.

Hush puppies are the usual accompaniment for fried catfish (see catfish). Deep-fry no more cakes than can float without crowding. Carefully use tongs to turn each cake several times as they bob up.

Serves 4 (8 hush puppies)

TORTILLAS

(Southwest)

1 cup cornmeal
1 cup all-purpose flour
1 teaspoon salt
3 tablespoons butter, or bacon drippings
1 cup lukewarm water

Place cornmeal in a mixing bowl and add flour sifted with salt. Using two dull knives or your fingers, work the butter (or bacon drippings) into the flour. Then knead with your fingers, adding water as required, until the dough ceases to stick to the bowl. Divide the dough into small balls of about a size that will fit loosely into the palm of your hand. Separate the balls with plastic wrap and refrigerate for 1/2 hour.

Flour a board and roll the dough on it until each ball is a thin round of about 5-1/2 inches.

Lightly grease a saucepan with butter or bacon drippings. When the fat is hot, place the tortillas in the pan and cook for 2 minutes on one side; turn, and cook for just over a minute on the other. Serve at once as an accompaniment to Spanish-inspired Southwest foods or as a base for enchiladas or tacos.

ENCHILADAS

(New Mexico)

1 pound cooked lean pork, ground
1/2 teaspoon chopped chili
1/2 small onion, minced
1/4 teaspoon garlic powder
1/2 teaspoon salt
freshly ground pepper
1/2 teaspoon cumin
1/4 teaspoon oregano
2 tablespoons cooking oil

Place the oil in a skillet over low heat, add all ingredients, and stir well until thoroughly blended. Remove from flame and spoon a little of the mixture into the center (from edge to edge) of each tortilla. Preheat oven to 275 degrees. Placed filled tortillas in a greased baking dish and bake for 15 minutes.

1/2 pound grated sharp cheddar cheese
2 tablespoons cooking oil

Blend cheese and oil in a saucepan and pour over enchiladas in baking pan. Increase oven heat to 350 degrees and bake for 20 minutes more.

RICE WAFFLES

(Southern)

In this authentic recipe a modern electric waffle iron is an excellent substitute for oldtime irons heated in hearths.

1/4 pound butter or margarine
1-1/4 cups flour
1 tablespoon sugar
3/4 tablespoon baking powder
1/2 teaspoon salt
1 cup cooked rice
3 eggs, separated
1 3/4 cups milk

Melt butter or margarine in a small saucepan over low heat. Heat waffle iron. Quickly sift flour with sugar, baking powder, and salt into a mixing bowl. Stir in cooked rice, melted butter, egg yolks, and milk. Beat until all ingredients are well blended. Beat egg whites in a separate bowl until stiffly peaked. The waffle iron is hot enough to use when a drop of water sprinkled on the grid sputters. Pour a dipper of batter on the grid and close the cover of the iron. Allow to bake for about 4-1/2 minutes, or the length of time suggested by the manufacturer's directions. Serve waffles hot with dabs of butter and maple or fruit syrup of your choice.

Serves 6

Cereals

FRIED OATMEAL SCRAPPLE

(Pennsylvania)

Much looked forward to on a cold winter morning, this fortified early-rising children for their walks to school, and adults for their hard chores.

1-1/2 cups uncooked oatmeal (quick or slow cooking)
1 teaspoon salt
2-3/4 cups water
1/2 cup fried bacon crumbs
oil, butter, or margarine

In a large deep saucepan, sprinkle oatmeal and salt into rapidly boiling water. Cook quick oatmeal 1 minute; slow cooking oats for 5 minutes. Remove from heat. Allow to stand uncovered 5 minutes, then stir in bacon crumbs. When mixture is well-congealed, turn into greased loaf pan. Cover tightly with plastic wrap, sealing all edges. Refrigerate for at least 8 hours. Cut into 1/2-inch thick pieces and pan fry in oil, butter, or margarine until well-browned. This will take about 12 minutes. Be sure to brown both sides. Serve with a dab of butter and use syrup of your choice for individual service. Another topping might be cinnamon and sugar combined. Eat with fork and knife for a delicious American breakfast.

Serves 4

FRIED CORNMEAL MUSH

(Pennsylvania and all points West)

5-1/2 cups water
1-1/4 cups cornmeal
1 teaspoon salt
1 egg yolk
2-1/2 tablespoons milk
4 slices bacon, fried and crumbled
2 tablespoons butter or margarine

Bring water to a boil in a deep saucepan over moderate heat. Reduce heat somewhat and gradually stir in cornmeal. Add salt and again raise heat until mixture boils. Cover and cook for 20 minutes. Pour thickened mixture into greased loaf pan and refrigerate until firm. Beat egg into milk and add bacon crumbs. Slice cornmeal mush and dip in egg-milk-bacon mixture. In a skillet, melt butter or margarine over low heat until sufficiently hot. Place coated mush slices in butter or margarine and brown on each side. Eat as is, or with warm fruit or maple syrup.

Serves 4 to 6

FARINA PUDDING

(Midwest)

1/2 cup farina
2 cups milk
3 tablespoons sugar
2 eggs, separated
fresh berries or sliced fruit
cream

In a deep saucepan over low heat, cook farina in milk, adding sugar and stirring occasionally, for 10 minutes. Remove from heat and beat yolks of eggs into mixture. In a small bowl, beat whites until moist and high. Fold into farina. If required, heat pudding over low flame for a minute or so. Serve with berries of choice as a topping and pour on cream for individual service.

Serves 4

HOMINY GRITS

(Southern)

Hominy grits are hulled, ground corn with the germ removed. In the early days of our country, this process was executed by hand. Today you may use the commercially prepared product.

1 cup hominy grits
1/4 cup light cream
1 teaspoon salt

Place grits, cream, and salt in the top of a double boiler. Cook 50 minutes, stirring occasionally.

Serve as a breakfast cereal with brown sugar and a dab of butter.

Serves 6

Desserts

SAFFRON RICE PUDDING

(Southern)

2 cups cooked rice
1 cup sugar
1/4 pound butter or margarine
1-1/2 teaspoons saffron
1 teaspoon cinnamon
2 tablespoons raisins
1 cup light cream
1/2 cup heavy cream, whipped

Combine all ingredients and cooked rice in a deep saucepan. Turn heat to low setting and stir ingredients well. Continue to stir until the cream is entirely absorbed. Serve warm with a dollop of whipped cream atop each portion.

Serves 4

DEL MONICO'S WHISPERS

(New Orleans)

These are as soft as a sigh and as fleeting on the tongue.

2/3 cup sifted all-purpose flour
1/4 teaspoon salt
2 tablespoons granulated sugar
2/3 cup cool (not cold) water
1/4 cup butter
3 eggs
1 teaspoon vanilla
1 tablespoon rum
oil for deep frying
2/3 cup confectioner's sugar

Sift flour, salt, and granulated sugar into a mixing bowl. Combine water and butter in a deep saucepan over low heat and stir until blended. Dump in flour mixture and stir vigorously until dough forms a pillow. Remove pot from heat and beat in eggs one at a time. Beat hard and continue to beat for 3 more minutes, add vanilla and rum, and mix thoroughly. Heat oil in a skillet over low heat. When the oil temperature reaches 350 degrees, or when a test dollop of dough browns and puffs in less than a minute, add teaspoonfuls of dough to oil. Brown, remove to paper toweling to drain, and cool somewhat. With a light touch, roll in confectioner's sugar. Serve warm.

Yields about 2 dozen puffs

LOG CABIN CUSTARD

(Illinois)

Custard, a time-honored American dessert, comes in many varieties and is known by many names. Nutritious and light, it is pleasant on the tongue and is a sliding-down-the-throat sort of dessert

On the frontier refined sugar, that unhealthful amenity of civilization, was hard to come by. Here is a recipe of improvisation.

2 cups milk
4 eggs
1/4 teaspoon salt
3 tablespoons honey
1-1/2 tablespoons molasses
1-1/2 teaspoons bourbon or whiskey

Preheat oven to 375 degrees. Cook milk in a deep saucepan over moderate heat until scalded. Remove from heat and, in a mixing bowl, beat eggs until lemon-colored. Beat in salt, honey, molasses, and hot milk. Continue beating, and add liquor, mixing well. Pour into 6 custard cups, and place cups in a pan of warm water. Bake for 40 minutes, or until the tines of a fork can be removed cleanly. Allow custard to cool at room temperature, then refrigerate for about 3 hours. Serve cold.

Serves 6

CREME BRULEE

(New Orleans)

Here is another sort of custard.

2 cups light cream
4 egg yolks
4 tablespoons granulated sugar
1 teaspoon vanilla extract
1/8 teaspoon salt
1 tablespoon brandy
1/2 cup brown sugar, sifted

Heat cream over boiling water in a double boiler. One at a time, beat egg yolks into cream and add granulated sugar, vanilla extract, salt, and brandy. Beat for 4 minutes. Preheat oven to 350 degrees. Pour into an 8 x 8-inch metal pan. Place this in a larger pan filled with warm water that does not reach the lip of the inner baking dish. Cover with a sheet of aluminum foil, being careful *not* to clamp down edges of foil. Bake for 30 to 40 minutes, or until tines of a fork can be removed cleanly. Cool at room temperature, then refrigerate for 5 to 6 hours. After removing from refrigerator, sprinkle brown sugar over all. Turn broiler heat on to 250 degrees. Place pan (must be metal) under heat. Broil for 2 minutes, or until sugar melts and caramelizes as a glaze. Remove from broiler and again refrigerate without room cooling. Refrigerate for about 1 hour.

Serves 4 to 6

SOFT CUSTARD ISLAND

(New England)

1 cup light cream
1 cup milk
4 tablespoons sugar
yolks of 4 eggs
1/8 teaspoon salt
1/4 teaspoon vanilla extract

Combine cream and milk in the top of a double boiler over boiling water. In a mixing bowl, beat sugar into egg yolks until frothy. Spoon in 1 cup of hot cream-milk mixture, then return all ingredients to double boiler. Continue to stir slowly but constantly until custard begins to thicken. Remove from heat and stir in salt and vanilla extract. At this time, any flavoring desired may be added (as 1 tablespoon of a concentrated fruit syrup.) Beat at low speed of mixer for about 30 seconds, or for 1 minute by hand. Cover bowl with plastic wrap, sealing edges, and refrigerate for 2 hours before serving.

Serves 3 to 4

BAKED BANANAS

(Hawaii)

4 tablespoons butter
1/2 cup brown sugar
1 tablespoon lemon juice
1/2 cup sherry
6 firm bananas, peeled

Melt butter in a skillet over low heat. Add sugar and lemon juice, then slowly add sherry. Preheat oven to 375 degrees. Halve bananas lengthwise and place in buttered baking dish, cut side up. Spoon syrup over bananas. Dot with butter and bake for about 18 minutes, or until bananas are softened.

Serves 6

BAKED PEARS

(Oregon)

2 large pears, or 4 small ones, washed and *not* pared
2 tablespoons honey
1 teaspoon grated lemon rind
1/4 teaspoon ground ginger
1 tablespoon butter or margarine
1/4 cup orange juice
2 tablespoons brandy

Preheat oven to 375 degrees. Place pears (seeded), cut side up, in greased baking dish. Spread pears with honey. Dust with grated lemon rind and ginger, and dot each pear with butter or margarine. Spoon orange juice over evenly, and then the brandy. Arrange metal foil loosely across the pan and bake for 50 minutes, or until pears are tender. Look at pears about 2 or 3 times during baking to see if they are moist enough. If needed, baste with added orange juice. Serve warm.

Serves 4

STRAWBERRY FRANGO

(California)

1 pint fresh strawberries, washed and hulled
3/4 cup milk
2 egg yolks
1/2 cup plus 1 tablespoon sugar
1 cup heavy cream

Crush berries in a blender or by mashing with a spoon. Heat milk in a saucepan over moderate heat until a skin just begins to form. Remove from heat. In a mixing bowl, beat egg yolks into sugar. Gradually dribble in a stream of milk, and continue to beat until all ingredients are well blended. Turn mixture into saucepan over low heat. Stir constantly until mixture congeals somewhat. Be careful not to allow it to boil so that it will not curdle. Pour into serving dishes and allow to cool at room temperature, then refrigerate for 30 minutes. Beat cream until it forms high peaks. Layer cream on top of custard. Place in freezer section of your refrigerator and freeze for at least 5 hours.

Serves 4

CARAMEL BANANAS

(Louisiana)

1 cup light brown sugar, packed
4 tablespoons heavy cream
1/2 cup butter or margarine
1/16 teaspoon salt
1 teaspoon vanilla
6 ripe bananas, peeled and cut lengthwise into halves
1 cup whipped cream

Preheat oven to 300 degrees. In a small saucepan over low heat, cook brown sugar, cream, butter or margarine, and salt until thickened. Do not allow to burn or boil. Remove from heat and add vanilla. Place bananas in a greased baking dish and pour hot sauce over. Bake for 10 minutes. Garnish with whipped cream just before service. One portion consists of two halves.

Serves 6

BREAD AND BUTTER PUDDING

(Midwest)

12 slices white bread, without crust
1/2 cup chopped citron
1/2 cup raisins

CUSTARD

1-1/2 quarts milk
6 eggs
1-1/2 cups sugar
1/8 teaspoon salt
1 tablespoon nutmeg
1 teaspoon vanilla

Preheat oven to 400 degrees. Line bottom and sides of a 2-quart baking dish with bread, after first greasing the dish. Arrange slices so that they overlap. Sprinkle on citron and raisins. Combine all custard ingredients in a saucepan over low heat. Simmer for about 8 minutes (do not allow to boil) and pour mixture over bread. Place baking dish in a pan of water and bake for 35 minutes. This may be served as is, or with a topping of chopped nuts or a sprinkling of cocoa.

Serves 6 to 8

BOURBON PUDDING

(Kentucky)

1 cup butter
2-1/2 cups sugar
3 tablespoons flour
4 egg yolks, well beaten
1 cup heavy cream
2 teaspoons orange juice
1/2 cup bourbon
1 teaspoon nutmeg
1 teaspoon grated orange peel

Preheat oven to 375 degrees. In the top of a double boiler, melt butter, and stir in sugar, mixing well. Gradually mix in flour, then egg yolks and heavy cream. Stir constantly. Add orange juice and bourbon. Remove from heat and turn into a greased 1-quart casserole. Top with a dusting of nutmeg and grated orange peel. Bake for 40 minutes, or until pudding is set. Serve hot or chilled.

Serves 4 to 6

INDIAN PUDDING

(New England)

5-1/2 cups milk
2/3 cup cornmeal
4 tablespoons honey
1/2 cup molasses
1/4 pound butter or margarine
3/4 teaspoon salt
1/8 teaspoon powdered cloves
3 tablespoons orange marmalade

Heat milk in a deep saucepan over moderate heat and gradually stir in cornmeal and all ingredients except marmalade. Allow to reach a boil, then lower heat and simmer for about 8 minutes. Stir constantly until creamy and thick. Preheat oven to 325 degrees. Turn mixture into 1-quart greased baking dish. Bake for 1-3/4 hours, when pudding should be nearly set. Spread marmalade across pudding and return to oven to bake 30 minutes longer. Serve warm, with cream if desired.

Serves 4 to 6

FLUMMERY

(South)

1/2 cup sugar
1/3 cup cornstarch
1/8 teaspoon salt
3 cups milk
2 egg yolks, lightly beaten
1 teaspoon rum extract

Combine 1/2 the sugar and all of the cornstarch and salt in a saucepan, and gradually pour in milk. Beat constantly, turn heat to moderate, and continue to beat constantly until mixture comes to a boil. As soon as mixture thickens, reduce heat to low. Beat egg yolks in a bowl and beat in a tablespoon of mixture. Slowly pour egg yolks into slowly cooking mixture. Do not allow to boil. Remove from heat and stir in rum extract. Cover with plastic wrap, sealing all edges of bowl, and refrigerate for about 3 hours, when flummery will be well chilled. Serve as is, or with fruit topping, chocolate sauce, or your favorite sauce.

Serves 4 or 5

APPLE CRISP

(Northeast)

3 cups pared, sliced apples (use firm cooking apples)
1 cup all-purpose flour
2 teaspoons baking powder
1-1/2 cups sugar
1/2 teaspoon salt
1-1/2 teaspoons cinnamon
1 teaspoon nutmeg
1 egg
1/4 pound melted butter or margarine
1 cup heavy cream, whipped

Preheat oven to 350 degrees. Place apple slices in a mixing bowl and sift in flour, baking powder, sugar, salt, cinnamon, and nutmeg. Beat well and break in egg, add melted butter, and continue to beat. Don't be concerned if apple slices are somewhat broken by beating process. Lightly grease baking dish, pour in mixture, and bake for 45 minutes. Serve warm with a dollop of whipped cream atop each serving.

Serves 6

SIOUX WASNI PUDDING

(Western)

1/3 cup bacon drippings
2 cups cornmeal
2/3 cup raisins
1/4 cup dates, pitted
1/2 cup pitted fresh cherries, halved
1 cup brown sugar
2 tablespoons honey

Lightly grease skillet with 1 tablespoon of bacon drippings. Immediately add cornmeal and stir in remaining bacon drippings and remaining ingredients. Cook over low heat, with constant stirring, for about 15 minutes, or until cornmeal has turned a deep golden color. Serve warm. (A spoonful of cherry brandy or liqueur might be spooned over each portion.)

Serves 6

AMBROSIA

(Alabama)

This dessert is popular at Christmas time and, in some families, is as traditional as holly wreaths.

4 medium oranges
2 medium bananas
1-1/2 cups moist shredded coconut
1/4 cup sugar
1/2 cup brandy

Peel, pit, and slice oranges. Peel and slice bananas. If you cannot obtain shredded sufficiently moist coconut, add 1 or 2 tablespoons milk to the coconut and mix well in a bowl before adding to other ingredients.

Combine oranges, bananas, coconut, and sugar in a large serving bowl. Pour brandy over all and gently mix through. Refrigerate until ready for use.

Serves 4 to 6

Sweet Baked Goods

PECAN KISSES

(Georgia)

2 egg whites
1/8 teaspoon salt
2/3 cup brown sugar
1/2 cup pecans, finely chopped
1 teaspoon rum blavoring

Preheat oven to 325 degrees. Beat egg whites until fairly stiff and add salt. Then gradually add brown sugar, pecans, and rum flavoring. Beat again to achieve stiffness.

Prepare cookie sheets by lining with brown paper (clean wrapping paper or a grocery bag, is fine). Drop spoonfuls of mixture onto paper and bake for 20 to 25 minutes. Loosen kisses with spatula or knife and allow to cool on platter.

Makes about 2 dozen cookies

APPLE PIE

(U.S.A., all the way!)

1 9-inch pie shell with dough for upper crust (unbaked)
6-1/2 cups pared, sliced apples
2/3 cup brown sugar
1/8 teaspoon salt
1-1/2 tablespoons cornstarch
1/3 teaspoon cinnamon
1/4 teaspoon nutmeg
1/8 teaspoon powdered cloves
2 tablespoons butter or margarine
1 teaspoon lemon juice
1 teaspoon vanilla

Line pie pan with dough (pie shell). Arrange apple slices in circular pattern, one piece overlapping the other. When bottom layer is complete, sprinkle over or dot with half of each of the following: brown sugar, salt, cornstarch, cinnamon, nutmeg, cloves, butter or margarine, lemon juice, and vanilla. Arrange remaining apple slices in a second (top) layer. Again, sprinkle over or dot with the remainder of the same ingredients. Preheat oven to 475 degrees. Cover pie filling with remaining dough (upper crust). Use the tines of a fork to create a design in the crust from which juices can escape. Bake for 7 minutes, then lower oven heat to 350 degrees. Bake for 50 minutes more, when crust should be nicely browned and pie fully baked.

KUCHEN

(Wisconsin)

The name is German for cake, but the recipe is purely American.

3-1/4 cups all-purpose flour
1-1/3 cups sugar
1 teaspoon salt
1 package yeast
1/4 cup warm water
1/2 teaspoon mace
1/16 teaspoon allspice
1/2 pound plus 1 tablespoon butter or margarine
3 egg yolks
3/4 cup warm water

Sift flour with sugar and salt into a mixing bowl. Place yeast in warm water. When yeast has dissolved, beat into the flour mixture. Add mace and allspice. Beat vigorously and add butter or margarine and, one at a time, the egg yolks. Stir in just enough of the water to make the batter of a smooth, pliable consistency. Cover bowl with a towel and let stand in a place without drafts for 1 hour, when dough should have doubled in size. Preheat oven to 350 degrees. Lightly grease two 8-inch square pans, and turn half of mixture into each. Bake for 30 minutes, when cakes should be nicely browned. Test with fork tines, which can be cleanly removed when cake is done.

SALLY LUNN

(Southern)

Betsy Ross is remembered for her stitchery, and the name of Sally Lunn lives on whenever this bread is baked. (Sometimes called by the designation of cake. If used as such, it could then be dusted with confectioner's sugar.)

4-1/4 cups all-purpose flour
1/3 cup sugar
1 teaspoon salt
1 package yeast
1-1/4 cups milk
1/4 pound butter or margarine
3 eggs

Sift flour into a mixing bowl with sugar and salt. Warm 1/4 cup of the milk and yeast. When yeast has dissolved, stir this into the mixture. Gradually stir in the remaining milk (unheated). Beat in butter or margarine and the eggs, one at a time. Beat by hand or mixer until dough is smooth and elastic. Lightly grease another bowl and turn dough into it. Cover bowl with a soft cloth and allow dough to rise in a warm, draftfree place. After 1 hour, dough will have doubled in bulk. Preheat oven to 400 degrees. Lightly grease and flour a 10-inch tube pan. Bake for 35 minutes, or until tines of a fork can be cleanly removed.

DATE-POTATO-NUT CAKE

(Texas)

3/4 cup shortening
2 cups brown sugar
3 eggs
1 cup cooked mashed potatoes, unseasoned
1-3/4 cups all-purpose flour
1 teaspoon salt
1-1/2 teaspoons baking soda
1 teaspoon ground cloves
1/2 teaspoon nutmeg
1/4 teaspoon allspice
3/4 cup dates, chopped
3/4 cup pecans, chopped, and unsalted
1 cup sour cream

Preheat oven to 325 degrees. In a mixing bowl, cream shortening and brown sugar. Add eggs and beat in well, then add mashed potatoes and sift in flour with salt, baking soda, cloves, nutmeg, and allspice. Continue beating and add chopped dates, pecans, and sour cream. Grease and lightly flour a loaf pan and turn mixture into it. Bake for 1 hour 10 minutes, or until cake is done. Test for doneness with tines of a fork. When tines can be inserted and cleanly removed, cake will be done. If further baking is required, check after about 6 minutes more for doneness.

SPICE CAKE

(Eastern)

Here's a short cut to a traditional favorite. No one will suspect that you cut corners.

1-1/2 cups packaged biscuit mix
1/2 cup sugar
1 egg
1/2 cup cold water
2 tablespoons melted butter or margarine
1 teaspoon vanilla
1/2 teaspoon allspice
1/4 cup butter or margarine
2/3 cup chopped nutmeats (unsalted)
1-1/4 cups confectioner's sugar

Preheat oven to 350 degrees. In a mixing bowl, combine biscuit mix, sugar, egg, water, melted butter or margarine, vanilla, and allspice. Beat for 4 minutes by hand or with a mixer on medium speed. Scrape bowl to mix all portions of batter thoroughly. Lightly grease an 8 x 8 x 2-inch pan and turn batter into pan. Bake for 35 minutes, or until the tines of a fork can be cleanly withdrawn. Also, the cake should spring back when lightly touched with a fingertip. Allow the cake to cool on a wire rack at room temperature. In a mixing bowl, beat butter into nutmeats. Add confectioner's sugar and continue to beat. Top the cooled cake with the nut mixture. Do not serve until entirely cool. Serving pieces should be square.

SPICE CAKE

(Western)

2 cups all-purpose flour
1 teaspoon baking powder
1 teaspoon baking soda
2/3 teaspoon salt
1 teaspoon cinnamon
1 teaspoon nutmeg
1 teaspoon allspice
1/2 teaspoon powdered cloves
3 eggs
1-2/3 cups dark brown sugar
1/4 pound butter or margarine
1 cup buttermilk
1/2 cup seeded prunes, chopped
1/2 cup dark raisins
1 cup chopped walnuts

Preheat oven to 375 degrees. Sift flour, baking powder, baking soda, salt, cinnamon, nutmeg, allspice, and powdered cloves into a mixing bowl. In a separate bowl, beat eggs and gradually mix them through the flour. In a bowl, mix brown sugar and butter or margarine, creaming well, and gradually beat into the mixture, along with the buttermilk. When all ingredients are well blended, mix through prunes, raisins, and walnuts. Turn into two 9-inch loaf pans and bake for 35 minutes, or until done. Cake is done when the tines of a fork can be cleanly removed after insertion. Allow to cool on a wire rack. When cool, frost.

FROSTING

1/4 pound butter or margarine
1 cup brown sugar
1/3 cup milk
1-1/4 cups confectioner's sugar

In a saucepan, melt the butter or margarine (cut into chunks), and gradually stir in brown sugar. Stir in the milk when the sugar is melted. Remove from heat and allow to cool at room temperature. Mix through confectioner's sugar and beat well. When mixture is smooth, apply frosting to loaves.

POTATO CAKE

(Far West)

2 cups sugar
1 cup shortening
1 cup mashed potatoes
4 eggs, separated
2 cups all-purpose flour
3 tablespoons cocoa
2 teaspoons baking powder
1 teaspoon cinnamon
1/2 teaspoon nutmeg
3/4 cup milk

FROSTING

2 tablespoons butter or margarine
1/2 cup smooth peanut butter
3 cups confectioner's sugar
4-1/2 tablespoons milk (more, if needed)

Cream sugar and shortening in a mixing bowl. Stir in potatoes, then egg yolks. Sift in flour, cocoa, baking powder, cinnamon, and nutmeg and add milk. Without prior beating, beat in egg whites. Continue beating well for at least 5 minutes or until batter is smooth. Grease three 9-inch layer pans. Preheat oven to 350 degrees. Turn mixture evenly into three pans and bake for 20 minutes, or until tines of a fork can be removed cleanly. While cakes are cooling on wire racks, combine frosting ingredients in a mixing bowl and mix well. If frosting is hard to manage, add a bit more butter and milk. When cakes are cool, frost the top of each layer, including the top of the cake. The sides need not be frosted.

RANCH DOUGHNUTS

(Utah)

4 cups all-purpose flour
1 tablespoon baking powder
1-1/2 teaspoons cinnamon
1/2 teaspoon nutmeg
3/4 teaspoon salt
2 eggs
1/2 pound melted butter
1 cup plus 1 tablespoon sugar
1 cup milk
oil for frying
1 cup confectioner's sugar

Sift flour with baking powder, cinnamon, nutmeg, and salt into a mixing bowl. In a separate bowl, beat eggs lightly and stir in melted butter, sugar, and milk. Gradually add flour to egg-sugar mixture, beating well, until all of flour has been added. Lightly flour a board and roll dough to a thickness of 1/2-inch. These are doughnuts without holes. With a cutter or the rim of a glass, cut doughnuts that are at least 2-1/2 inches in diameter. Discard scraps. Rolling the dough again toughens it. Cover with plastic wrap and refrigerate for about 1 hour. Heat oil to 375 degrees and deep-fry doughnuts (as many at a time as your frying pan will accommodate). Remove when browned and puffed. This will require about 3 minutes frying time. Drain on paper toweling. Cool at room temperature. Dust with confectioner's sugar.

Yields about 18 doughnuts

BOURBON PIE

(Kentucky)

This recipe comes from the state where they would be pleased to drink their juleps and then use more of the same bourbon in their dessert pie.

6 egg yolks
3/4 cup sugar
1 envelope unflavored gelatin
1/4 cup warm water
1/3 cup plus 1 tablespoon bourbon
1 teaspoon vanilla extract
1/16 teaspoon salt
1 pint heavy cream
1 baked 9-inch pie shell
mint sprigs

In a mixing bowl, beat egg yolks into sugar. Beat for at least 4 minutes. Sprinkle gelatin into warm water and allow to stand until gelatin dissolves. Pour this into the egg-sugar mixture and continue to beat. Add bourbon, vanilla extract, and salt, and beat these ingredients in until thoroughly blended. In a small bowl, beat cream until softly peaked. Fold cream into mixture in larger bowl, blend well, and spoon into pie shell. Place decorative sprigs of mint across the top. Place pie, uncovered, in refrigerator for 7 to 8 hours.

SWEET POTATO PIE

(Southern)

3 pounds sweet potatoes
1 cup heavy cream
1/2 cup milk, scalded
2/3 cup brown sugar
1 teaspoon nutmeg
1/2 teaspoon cinnamon
1/4 teaspoon allspice
1/2 teaspoon salt
2 eggs
1-1/4 tablespoons grated orange peel
1 prepared 9-inch pie shell, unbaked
2 tablespoons melted mutter

Peel potatoes, cut into pieces, and place in a deep saucepan with water to a depth of about 1-1/2 inches. Boil over moderate heat for 30 to 35 minutes. Drain.

Preheat oven to 425 degrees. Sieve potatoes into a mixing bowl and stir in cream and milk. Add brown sugar, nutmeg, ginger, cinnamon, allspice, and salt and stir through. In a bowl, beat eggs lightly and mix orange peel into the eggs. Slowly stir this into the potato mixture. When all ingredients are well blended, turn the mixture into a pie shell. With a pastry brush, lightly go over the filling with melted butter.

Bake for 15 minutes, then reduce heat to 350°

and bake for 45 to 40 minutes more. Pie is done when the tines of a fork can be cleanly removed.

1 cup heavy cream
1/4 cup brandy

Beat cream until stiffly peaked, and gradually stir brandy through. Cover pie with cream and serve warm or chilled.

SHOOFLY PIE

(Pennsylvania Dutch)

This is not a pie at all, but a molasses coffee-type cake baked in a pie shell.

PASTRY

1-1/2 cups all-purpose flour
1/2 teaspoon salt
1/2 cup shortening
3 tablespoons cold water

Sift flour and salt into a mixing bowl. Add shortening and work it through with two dull knives until the dough separates into pealike pieces. Sprinkle over the cold water and shape dough into a ball. Cover lightly with plastic wrap and refrigerate for 1/2 hour. Then flour a board and roll dough to a size to fit a 9-inch pan, with 1 inch of overlap. Line pan with dough and set aside.

CRUMBS

2 cups sifted flour
2/3 cup sugar
1/3 cup butter
1/8 teaspoon salt

Blend all ingredients in a mixing bowl with your fingers until fine crumbs form.

1/2 teaspoon baking soda
1/2 cup molasses
1/2 cup boiling water
1 egg yolk
2/3 of the crumbs

Preheat oven to 400 degrees. In a mixing bowl, add baking soda to molasses and stir in the boiling water until the mixture foams. Beat in egg yolk. Add 2/3 of the crumbs and turn mixture into pie shell. Spread remaining crumbs as a topping. Bake for 10 minutes. Lower heat to 350° and bake for 25 minutes longer, or until crumbs and crust are a golden brown.

KEY LIME PIE

(Florida)

Following the South's defeat in the Civil War, condensed milk, then a relatively new product, was widely used throughout the impoverished southern states as an inexpensive form of milk. It was in Key West that it became part of a renowned pie recipe.

4 eggs, separated
1 can condensed milk
3/4 cup fresh lime juice
1 prebaked pie shell
3/4 cup sugar

Preheat oven to 450 degrees. In a mixing bowl, beat egg yolks into condensed milk, gradually add lime juice, and continue to beat for five minutes more. When it has thickened turn filling into pie shell. In a separate bowl, beat egg whites until they are stiff and peaked. Gradually work in sugar. Cover filling with meringue and bake for about 6 or 7 minutes, when meringue peaks should be slightly tinged a golden-brown. Allow to cool at room temperature on wire rack. Do *not* refrigerate.

WALNUT DUMPLINGS

(Virginia)

1 cup brown sugar
2 cups all-purpose flour
2-1/2 teaspoons baking powder
1/16 teaspoon salt
1 teaspoon cinnamon
1 cup milk
1 egg, well beaten
1 teaspoon melted butter or margarine
1 cup chopped walnuts (unsalted)
2 cups brown sugar
1 cup water
1 teaspoon melted butter or margarine

Preheat oven to 375 degrees. Into a mixing bowl, sift brown sugar, flour, baking powder, salt, and cinnamon. Beat in milk, then beaten egg and melted butter or margarine. When dough is smooth, stir in the walnuts. In a saucepan over low heat, combine brown sugar, water, and melted butter or margarine. Stir well and do not allow to burn. When boiling point is reached, allow to boil for 2-1/2 minutes. During this time, add batter to the boiling sauce while stirring rapidly. Turn mixture into a greased pan, apportioning batter into 8 equal-size dumplings with sides not touching. Bake for 25 minutes and check for brownness. When dumplings are fully brown and crisp on the outside, they are done.

MATRIMONIAL CAKE

(Southern)

2 cups brown sugar
2 pounds dates, chopped
1/2 cup hot water
1/2 pound butter or margarine
2 cups all-purpose flour
3 cups quick oatmeal
1 teaspoon baking soda
1 teaspoon salt

Combine brown sugar, dates, and water in a saucepan over moderate heat. Cook for 25 minutes, stir, mashing somewhat as you do, and continue to cook for 15 minutes more. Allow to cool. Preheat oven to 325 degrees. In a mixing bowl, cream butter or margarine and sift flour into this, then, stirring quickly, beat in oatmeal and add baking soda and salt. Continue to beat for 5 full minutes. Grease a square 9 x 9-inch baking pan. Bake for 40 minutes, when cake should be brown. Test for doneness with the tines of a fork. If inserted tines can be removed cleanly, cake is done. Allow to cool at room temperature. After 30 minutes, remove cake to a wire rack, and continue cooling for 2 hours more. Serve in square pieces.

PECAN PIE

(Georgia)

If Georgia had an official state pie, this would be it.

2/3 cup pecan halves, unsalted
1 cup chopped pecans, unsalted
3 tablespoons butter or margarine
3/4 cup sugar
2 tablespoons molasses
2 tablespoons honey
1 teaspoon vanilla extract
3 eggs
3/4 cup dark corn syrup
1/2 teaspoon salt
1 unbaked pie shell (9 inch)

Preheat oven to 450 degrees. Hold pecan halves in reserve and, in a mixing bowl, combine chopped pecans with butter or margarine and cream well. Beating constantly, gradually stir in sugar, molasses, honey, and vanilla extract. In a separate bowl, beat eggs well and gradually stir the beaten eggs into the pie filling mixture. When this has been thoroughly blended, stir in corn syrup and season with salt. Turn pie filling into unbaked shell and arrange pecan halves across the top. Bake for 12 minutes, then reduce heat to 350 degrees. Continue baking for 40 minutes more, or until pie is done. Test by inserting tines of a fork into filling. When tines can be cleanly removed, pie is done. Cool on wire rack before serving.

Confections

STUFFED PRUNES

(California)

2 dozen prunes, pitted
1 cup chopped walnuts
2 tablespoons honey
1 tablespoon butter or margarine
1/2 cup confectioner's sugar

Spread prunes apart to receive filling and place in readiness on working board. In a small bowl, combine chopped walnuts, honey, and butter or margarine. Stuff prunes with mixture. Roll each prune in confectioner's sugar.

Yields 2 dozen

PEANUT BRITTLE

(Virginia)

Actually the peanut is a vegetable, not a nut. The confectioner's recipe was originated long ago.

2 cups brown sugar, tightly packed
1/2 cup granulated sugar
1 cup light corn syrup
1/3 cup plus 1 tablespoon water
1-3/4 cups peanuts, roasted, shelled, and unsalted
1 tablespoon butter
1-1/4 teaspoons vanilla
1/4 teaspoon salt
1-1/2 teaspoons baking soda

In a deep saucepan over low heat, combine brown sugar, granulated sugar, corn syrup, and water. Stir well. Cook mixture until a candy thermometer registers 230 degrees, or until a little dropped from the tip of a spoon forms a thread in a cup of cold water. Stir in peanuts and butter, and continue to cook without stirring until thermometer registers 315 degrees, or until a drop from a spoon into a cup of cold water forms a *brittle* thread. At this point, remove pot from heat and quickly stir in vanilla, salt, and baking soda. Pour a thin layer into a well-creased flat pan, or onto greased, flat platters. Allow to cool thoroughly at room temperature. Break into uneven, jagged pieces.

Yields about 1-1/2 pounds

CAMPUS FUDGE

(Midwest)

2 cups sugar
1/2 cup cocoa
1/2 cup butter
2 cups cream
1/16 teaspoon salt
1 teaspoon vanilla

Combine sugar and cocoa in a deep saucepan over low heat. Stirring constantly, add butter and blend well. Stir in the cream and salt. Increase heat very slightly and stir constantly. Candy is done when a candy thermometer registers 238 degrees, or when a drop from the tip of a spoon into a cup of cold water forms a soft ball. Remove fudge pot from heat and place in a deep pan filled with cold water. Cover pot. After 15 minutes, beat fudge until smooth and thick. Add vanilla. Lightly grease a shallow pan and pour fudge into this. Allow about 6 hours to harden. Cut into squares.

Yields about 1 pound

PRALINES

(Creole)

This is a Creole confection, originally made with almonds for the enjoyment of a man named Praslin. In time, the substitution of pecans was effected, and the affinity of pecans for brown sugar has become history.

3 cups light brown sugar
1 tablespoon butter
1/3 cup water
2-1/2 cups pecans, halved

In a saucepan over low heat, combine light brown sugar, butter, and water. Insert candy thermometer. When it registers 234°, or when sugar syrup dropped from the tip of a spoon into a cup of cold water forms a soft ball, add pecans and stir carefully so as not to break nuts. After 3-1/2 minutes, remove from heat and continue to stir the mixture as it grows thicker. To form pralines, spoon a large spoonful onto wax paper, forming flat round pralines about 2-1/2 inches around.

Yields about 2 dozen

PECAN DROPS

(Mississippi)

A traditional confection from the heart of the deep South. Although these are baked, they are more candy than cookie.

1 egg white, stiffly beaten
1 cup light brown sugar
1-3/4 cups pecan halves (unsalted)

Preheat oven to 250 degrees. Lightly grease baking sheet. Gradually beat brown sugar into stiffly beaten egg yolks. This makes a dull-appearing meringue. Very gently fold in pecan halves. Drop meringue by teaspoonfuls onto the baking sheet. Do not allow these to touch as they will expand slightly during baking. Bake for 35 minutes, or until candies will be firm and have a pale tan shade.

Yields about 2 dozen

BOARDWALK SALTWATER TAFFY

(Atlantic City)

Three things are usually associated with Atlantic City—the boardwalk, the rolling surf, the saltwater taffy.

1 cup sugar
2/3 tablespoon cornstarch
3/4 cup light corn syrup
1/2 cup water
1/2 teaspoon salt
flavorings: peppermint, chocolate, almond, orange, strawberry, and vanilla extracts
1 tablespoon butter or margarine

Blend sugar and cornstarch in a saucepan over low heat and stir in corn syrup. Increase heat to moderate and, continuing to stir, add water and salt. Insert a candy thermometer. When it registers 252 degrees or when a drop of syrup dropped from the tip of a spoon into a cup of cold water forms a solid ball, remove from heat and pour into a greased bowl. Immediately blend in flavor extract. Do this for as many flavors as you wish. Pour taffy onto greased pan and allow to cool. Later, with buttered hands, pull the taffy pieces until they are each elongated and springy. Mold a 1-inch thick rope and cut off 1-1/2 inch pieces with scissors. Allow to cool and further set. Then wrap each piece in foil or wax paper.

Yields nearly a pound

Beverages

EGG LEMONADE

(Ohio, Shaker)

2 eggs
4 teaspoons sugar
2/3 cup lemon juice
5 cups cold water
sprigs of mint

In a bowl, lightly beat eggs and sugar. Add lemon juice and mix through. Place cold water in a pitcher and add mixture, blending well. Refrigerate until use. Garnish each serving with a mint sprig.

Serves 6

SPICED HOT CHOCOLATE

(New Mexico)

4 ounces (4 squares) chocolate, grated
1/2 cup milk
1-1/2 cups milk
1 teaspoon vanilla
1/4 cup brown sugar (granulated)
1/2 teaspoon cinnamon
1/4 teaspoon nutmeg
dash of cloves (powdered)
2 tablespoons light rum
dash of salt

In the top of a double boiler, heat the chocolate and milk, stirring constantly until the chocolate is melted.

Gradually add the remaining ingredients to the melted chocolate, stirring constantly. When all ingredients are blended and drink is heated to just below boiling temperature, serve it in small cups, much as demitasse coffee.

Serves 4 to 6

HOT BUTTERED RUM

(New England)

Traditional on a cold wintry night, this is as satisfying today as in Colonial times.

4 cups apple cider or apple juice
2-1/2 tablespoons brown sugar
1-1/2 teaspoons butter or margarine
1/3 cup Jamaica rum
1/2 teaspoon lemon juice
4 cinnamon sticks

Heat cider in a saucepan over moderate heat until very hot but not boiling. Stir in sugar, then butter, and cook until these melt. Keeping heat low, add rum and lemon juice, stirring once. Serve immediately in large mugs or tall glasses. Be sure, if you use glasses, that you place a teaspoon in each glass when you pour in the hot beverage. Place a cinnamon stick in each mug or glass.

Serves 4

RASPBERRY SHRUB

(Southern)

The Southern summer heat made it necessary to devise many refreshing beverages. One used throughout the South was the shrub.

SYRUP

1 quart red or black raspberries (washed)
1/2 pint apple cider vinegar
1-3/4 cups sugar

Combine all syrup ingredients in a heavy saucepan and simmer over medium heat. When sugar dissolves, increase heat and boil, uncovered, for 5 minutes. Skim off foam. Remove to covered container and store in refrigerator for 2 days. This allows the ingredients to mellow together.

2/3 glass ice water
1/3 glass shrub syrup
ice cubes
sprigs of mint

Combine above ingredients and syrup. Serve in tall glasses.

Yields 8 to 10 glassfuls

SYLLABUB

(Virginia)

This drink was a favored refreshment in Colonial times. In fact, in proper society, there was a special cone-shaped footed glass for syllabub. Today a juice glass or large wine glass will suffice.

3/4 cup milk
1/2 cup light cream
1 cup apple cider (if you prefer, substitute red or white wine)
2 tablespoons heavy, sweet fruit syrup of your choice

Pour milk, cream, and cider (or wine) into a pitcher or a deep bowl. Allow mixture to sit at room temperature for 1 hour. Beat well with a wire whisk or electric mixer and stir in fruit syrup. The drink is thick, approaching the consistency of soft curd.

Serves 8

SPARKLING PUNCH

(Florida)

3 cups water
3 tablespoons strong tea
1/2 cup light corn syrup
2 quarts orange juice
1/2 cup lime juice
1 quart carbonated water
2 oranges, washed and sliced with peel intact (seeded)
1 dozen large strawberries, sliced
fresh mint leaves
1 pint orange sherbert (optional)

Boil water in a large saucepan. Remove from heat and stir in tea, corn syrup, orange juice, lime juice, and carbonated water. Refrigerate. Pour into punch bowl, add oranges, and serve in tall glasses (unlike you usual punch) with ice cubes in each glass. Top each serving with strawberries and a sprig of mint. Serve as is or with a scoop of orange sherbert half over the rim of each glass.

Serves 12

TEXAN ICED TEA

(Texas)

One universal beverage that the hot, Texas climate has promoted is iced tea, very sweet and spicy. In Texas, a hostess not serving iced tea is regarded with some amazement.

3 tea bags
4 cups boiling water
4 tablespoons sugar
1/4 teaspoon allspice
4 sticks cinnamon
4 orange slices

Place tea bags in a bowl and pour boiling water over them. When tea is a rich color, remove bags and stir in sugar and allspice. Pour into container or pitcher and refrigerate until cold. Serve in tall glasses with ice cubes and insert a stick of cinnamon in each glass. Affix half of each orange slice to the rim of the glass.

Serves 4

SWITCHEL

(New England, Shaker)

The men haying in the fields were refreshed by great drafts of this beverage.

4-1/2 cups cold water
1 cup vinegar
1-1/4 cups brown sugar
1/2 cup molasses
1 teaspoon powdered ginger
2 teaspoons maple syrup

Mix all of the ingredients in a large bowl or pitcher. Refrigerate and serve.

Serves 6 to 8

HOT TODDY

(Ohio)

6 eggs
1/4 cup brown sugar
1 cup brandy or rum
5 cups boiling water
2 tablespoons lemon juice

Beat eggs and brown sugar in a large bowl. Stir in brandy or rum and gradually add boiling water, mixing well. Stir in lemon juice. Serve in heated mugs.

Serves 6

Index